A GUIDE FOR CATHOLIC WOMEN

W0010598

saying yes!

RESPONDING TO GOD'S INVITATION
TO **TRANSFORM** AND **ENERGIZE** OUR LIVES

KRISTIN ARMSTRONG AND **SALLY ROBB**

TWENTY-THIRD PUBLICATIONS
twentythirdpublications.com

TWENTY-THIRD PUBLICATIONS
One Montauk Avenue, Suite 200
New London, CT 06320
(860) 437-3012 or (800) 321-0411
www.twentythirdpublications.com

Cover photo: ©shutterstock.com/Fursov Maksim
Kristin Armstrong photo (page 4 & backcover) courtesy of Korey Howell.
Sally Robb photo (page 5 & backcover) courtesy of Amy Melsa.

ISBN: 978-1-62785-348-4
Library of Congress Control Number: 2017959388
Printed in the U.S.A.

 A division of Bayard, Inc.

CONTENTS

INTRODUCTION

We're so glad you said *yes* to opening this book.

Our initial *yes* to this project began when we agreed to write and teach a study for our local church in Austin, Texas. We spent many afternoons together, having coffee and sitting at Kristin's kitchen island with books, Bibles, and personal journals stacked around us. We are both Catholic girls, with faiths forged through life's fires as well as through stained glass windows. As Catholic girls, we love Mary and regard her as a role model of devotion and unconditional love. She was a simple Jewish girl with an uncomplicated, unwavering faith. When an angel approached her with the biggest maternal responsibility in history, carrying the Son of God as her child, her response was profound. Her *yes* changed the world.

We believe that God continues to ask women of faith big questions and present us with awesome opportunities, yet so often we hesitate or play small. We withhold our *yes* from God, and from the world. It is our hope that these chapters will offer introspection and inspiration into the particular ways that God is calling on you, today, in this season of your life. Your *yes* matters very much.

What we have found is that our *yes* is personal, but in learning to say *yes*, we also need each other. Spiritual writer Fr. Jacques Philippe once wrote of our need for "the mediating look of the other." He said it was like a plain girl, who has always just thought she was no one special, no one worth really "seeing." Then, one day, she falls in love, and for the first time, she knows that she is beautiful! God sees us as immensely beautiful, but sometimes that's hard to really take in. We need each other in order to help us "see." We need to stand as sisters, and help speak this beauty into being. "Benedicere," in Latin, means to speak well of someone. We should be a benediction, a blessing, to each other by recognizing and naming what is so good, so beautiful, in the sister who stands next to us. Very often, it will be the first time she has ever felt this "mediating look of love." We hope that this small work can be part of his "mediating look," a blessing that helps you see the truth of your beauty, value and calling.

Each chapter is based on a theme. Some of the themes came from our original lesson plans, but others came to us through our class discussions and interactions. Each theme represents an area of life where God might be asking us for our *yes*. In much the same organic way that we collaborated as we taught our class, each chapter contains an essay written by each of us. It is our hope that our different perspectives, life experiences, and styles of writing and teaching will resonate with your hearts and spirits in personal and unique ways.

It is an honor to think that perhaps our *yes* might inspire yours.

May God guide you and bless you all along the way,

Kristin and Sally

KRISTIN ARMSTRONG

 Hi, I'm Kristin. Kristin Cate Richard Armstrong, to be more precise.

Some people have very strong faith, and it seems they were just born that way. Others have to wrestle to get there. I'm a wrestler, I guess.

My father was Catholic and my mom was Lutheran. When it was time for me to get confirmed, I wasn't ready. When I was sixteen, after a hard first week at a new school, I stopped by to talk to my parish priest and everything changed. I said *yes* to my faith, finally, and I really meant it. I went through RCIA that year.

After that was college, work, marriage, three darling babies, and one painfully public divorce. In the wreckage, I had a chance for a life remodel. I took a leap of faith and started a dream career as a writer, giving volume to the voice I relegated to my journals for so many years. Seven, now eight, books later, and I am still saying *yes*.

I am a mother, a student, a teacher, a speaker, a writer, and a runner. I am passionate about helping women navigate transition zones, opening their hearts and minds to what God has in store for them on the other side of "this." Learning to say *yes* is a big part of that.

I look forward to sharing my heart and this journey.

SALLY ROBB

I came from a vibrant, but breakable, Catholic family. We moved from New Orleans, to war-torn Algiers, and then to Paris, dusty West Texas, and finally Alaska. Along the way, my parents divorced, married other people, and had other children. My childhood was full of energy and life, but it was also chaotic and difficult to navigate. So I fashioned a life inside myself. I read, and the edges of the world were pushed back. I played the piano for hours, and I felt like I was learning a language larger than words. Shot through everything was a certainty that God was immense and beautiful. I wanted to live into the largeness I saw in him.

I went to Yale, graduated, got married, and had six kids. Along the way, I got a Master's in theology. I taught high school seniors and then co-hosted two popular shows on Catholic radio, Morning Air and Mary's Touch. Now I teach classes and give retreats and conferences. But mostly I'm a mother. I hung my degrees over my washing machine, laughing at the thought that, for lots of time and money, you too can know when to put in the Downy! I get to live into God's largeness and beauty every day, because I found him planted right in the middle of the ordinary. Now, when the kitchen's full of dirty dishes, I know Jesus is waiting for me at the sink.

saying yes to
WORTHINESS

KRISTIN

Years ago I hung a white, painted cross above my girls' full-length closet mirror. On the cross is written a portion of Psalm 139, "For I am fearfully and wonderfully made." My intention was that every time they check themselves out with the question, "Do I look okay? Am I good enough?" I wanted them to see God's answer, right in front of them. How much anguish and unhappiness could we save ourselves (and each other) if we simply understood and embraced the truth that we are all wonderfully made, we are all made in the image and likeness of God, we are all *daughters of the King?*

Being a daughter of the King settles the epic identity questions *Who Am I?* and *Am I Worthy?* When the angel Gabriel visits Mary, he says to her, "Do not be afraid, Mary, for you have found favor with God." We often think we are unworthy of God's favor. And we often underestimate how much fear that causes. If an angel said to me, "Do not be afraid, Kristin, for you have found favor with God," I would bawl my eyes out. And not just because an angel came to see me. They would be tears of relief, a lifetime's worth. And maybe, at long last, I would truly stop being afraid. I can't even imagine all I could be and do if I truly grasped my identity and worthiness in Christ and ditched my fear.

Understanding our own worthiness is everything,

because until we do, we will chase every false god, every dead end, every detour, and every counterfeit in the world. We will sell ourselves short, and sell ourselves out. We will do and be and accept less than what was prepared for us. *Unworthiness is one of the key oppressive tactics of the enemy— particularly in inhibiting women of God.* A therapist once said to me, after I had had a particularly nasty breakup post-divorce, "You remind me of a crow. You chase what you think is shiny, even if it's really just a scrap of tinfoil." Ouch. Enough of that, already. If the enemy can make us believe that we aren't strong enough, smart enough, capable enough, good or godly enough, brave enough, skilled enough, and have enough time, then we will always shrink back and play small. This is exactly the enemy's point— unworthiness minimizes us more quickly and efficiently than anything else because it's an *inside job*. When we play small, we leave gaping holes in God's Kingdom plan where our contribution was meant to go. In the hole created by our absence, love goes out and fear comes in. Opportunities are lost. People who need God's love go unseen or unnoticed.

I battled unworthiness for longer than I care to admit. The perceived "failure" of my divorce whispered messages to me that became part of my belief system and caused me some painful delays and damages. Things like, "I am not enough." Or, "I am not worth fighting for." Perhaps you can think of some of your own messages, words that you have mistakenly incorporated into your beliefs. *I am not smart enough, pretty enough, thin enough, young enough, old enough, compelling enough, interesting enough. I don't have enough time, money, education, or confidence. I cannot be forgiven.* Women are susceptible to so many of these lies. These are all messages of scarcity, yet we serve a God of abundance. These are all messages of failure, yet we serve a God of redemption. These are all messages of comparison, yet we serve a God of unlimited and unconditional Love. These are all messages of condemnation and critique, yet we serve a God of mercy. These are all messages of defeat, yet we serve a victorious Savior.

I have to be so bold to ask: *What are we doing, ladies?*

Jesus says the most important commandments are "You shall love the Lord your God with all your heart, all your soul and all your mind, and you shall love your neighbor *as yourself.*" This statement assumes that we actually love ourselves. So, do we? Do we really? If we don't sort out our issues of identity and worthiness we can never truly love ourselves. Which means we can never really love anyone else, either.

And I don't know about you, but to me, a life story without a love story isn't much of a story at all.

I want you to do something for me. A little exercise that I like to call the Antivenom Exercise, because I believe it counteracts the poison of false beliefs. If you really do it, you cannot help but be changed. I want you to write down three to five false beliefs, lies you may have believed about yourself. Maybe someone said these words to you, or maybe you made them up all by yourself. It doesn't matter where they came from because ultimately they came from the dark. And now we're going to put them in the light (and fry them).

Next, I want you to spend some time (it may take a few days, so do it carefully) finding Scripture verses that counteract these lies and false beliefs with the Truth of God's Word. For example, my own "I am not worth fighting for" cannot stand in the face of Jeremiah 31:3—"I have loved you with an everlasting love; therefore I have continued my faithfulness to you." It withers in the light of Isaiah 41:10— "I will strengthen you and help you; I will uphold you with my righteous right hand." These words are direct from God, blowing clear through my little story that I am somehow not worth fighting for. These verses are healing balms, whispering to my soul, *Kristin, dear daughter, of course you are worth fighting for! I, the Creator of the Universe and Savior of the World and Master of Heaven and Earth, have been fighting for you all along.* This thought makes me smile. It also makes me feel rather worthy. Important even. Adored. Cherished. Like the beloved daughter that I am— that we all are.

Now it's your turn.

> I am the apple of God's eye. I am the righteous-
> ness of God. I am walking in the Kingdom. I am
> a joint heir with Christ. I am forgiven as far as the
> east is from the west. I am written in the book of
> life, across God's hand. I am God's workmanship.
> I am a person who has been given a spirit of power
> and of love and of a calm and well-balanced mind
> and discipline and control. I am able to do all things
> through Christ who strengthens me. I am fearfully

and wonderfully made. I turn my face to God and
am radiant. I am beauty from ashes. I am a daughter
of the King. I can be still and know that he is God.

I love the way Emmett Fox describes the "workroom," or
the "hidden studio of the mind." The mind is where the
beliefs reside that need to be strengthened or changed.
Changing the way we think changes the way we feel, which
changes the way we act (the way we act towards ourselves
and others as well as every decision we make). We make
entirely different choices from the standpoint of a foun-
dation of worthiness. This is how we change our lives. We
begin by counteracting lies with the Truth of God's Word.
We begin by thinking thoughts of worthiness. We begin
with our identity as a daughter of the King.

And do not be conformed to this world, but "be transformed by the renewing of your mind" (Romans 12:2).

SALLY

"**B**e transformed by the renewing of your mind." Will we allow God to speak this "new" word to us? Will we hear it and let it in? This word was spoken to Jesus at his baptism, and the Father speaks it to us, if we will only listen and let it in. "This is my beloved Son, on whom my favor rests" (Matthew 3:16–17; Mark 1:1–10; Luke 2:21–22). You are his beloved. His favor rests on you, and his grace is all around you! But we have listened so long to the world saying, "You are not enough." The messages Kristin describes, ones of comparison, scarcity, failure, condemnation, and defeat, are the ones we most often hear. The tragedy is that we believe them. I have seen women be kind and understanding to others, accepting their weaknesses, but be absolutely brutal with themselves. I know this, because this has so often been me. I heard someone ask one time, "If a friend spoke to you the way you speak to yourself, how long would they be your friend?" Not long, I think.

The discovery of our belovedness is one of the greatest gifts of the spiritual life. We come upon the startling recognition that God is a Father, a Creator, a lover, not a condemning judge waiting for us to stumble so that we are reminded of our weakness, our shame, our worthlessness. The only way to counteract those words of rejection and condemnation is to let God replace them with his words of life and mercy, words that reveal the deep and beautiful truth of our worthiness. Fr. Henri Nouwen took Scripture and wrote what God speaks to us in the center of our selves:

> "I have called you by name, from the very begin-
> ning. You are my Beloved, and on you my favor
> rests. I have carved you in the palms of my hands
> and hidden you in the shadow of my embrace.
> I have counted every hair on your head. Wherever
> you go, I go with you, and wherever you rest,
> I keep watch. You belong to me....wherever you are
> I will go. Nothing will ever separate us, for you and
> I are one." (*Life of the Beloved*, p. 36)

Speak these words over and over to yourself. Let them penetrate the darkness of your self-doubt. They are God's words to you, the words he wishes you to hold and believe. He sees you. He knows you. He knows everything about you. And he loves you. You are his beloved. We do not need to earn his love, because it is his love that brought us into being. He is not surprised, or disappointed, by our weakness and sin. He sees what has made us ashamed, and what has made us feel unworthy. He longs to heal us and make us whole, not to "satisfy Divine justice," but to show us the depth of his mercy and his love—mercy that lets us breathe, and love that brings us life.

In the fifth chapter of Mark's gospel, Jesus is on his way to heal Jairus' daughter. He's being followed closely by a crowd, pushing all around him. The woman with the hemorrhage, hearing about Jesus, leaves the isolation she has lived in for twelve years and, pressing forward, she reaches out to "touch the hem of his cloak" and is healed. Jesus stops, and he says, "Who touched me?" She falls at his feet and "tells him the whole truth." He says, "My daughter, your faith has healed you, go in peace and be free." There is so much that is beautiful there: her courage in leaving her isolation (the shame that kept her alone for so long); her effort and perseverance in "pressing forward" to touch Mercy (how easily we get discouraged, instead of "pressing forward"); her falling at his feet and opening to him the whole truth of her heart and life (the willingness to be vulnerable in front of Love); and finally, the gift he gives is not simply the healing; it is peace and freedom!

It is no coincidence that Jesus then enters the house of Jairus and is told, "The daughter is dead...." Jesus responds, "Don't be afraid; only have faith." There is a lot of commotion and drama. He tells them, "She is only asleep," and they mock him. He doesn't respond but takes the mother and the father into the girl's room. Going over to her, he takes her hand and whispers, "*Talitha kum!*" "Little one, arise!" She gets off the bed and walks around, and Jesus says, "Give her something to eat," because his love is powerful and practical.

The woman with the hemorrhage had been isolated and alone in her anguish. She had the courage to "come out" to find healing. She pressed forward, making the deliberate effort to "touch" Mercy. She was healed of the hemorrhage, but I think a deeper healing happened when she knelt at Love's feet and told him "her whole story." That became the completion of the healing; his look and his touch of infinite mercy meant she could "Go in peace and freedom"—freedom from the isolation of shame, peace that quiets the voices that call her "unclean," unworthy. Then he goes to raise the dead little girl.

The truth of our worthiness is revealed in both of these stories. We are the woman isolated, ashamed, and unworthy. We are the little girl, dead in our hurt, our trauma, our sin. Jesus comes to bring mercy, healing, peace, freedom, and life. He listens to "our whole story." He whispers "*Talitha kum,*" "arise, dear one," to what feels dead in us. He does not tell us we are wrong or deluded. The truth is an essential part of accepting our worthiness, because our worthiness is a part of our Be-ing, not a product of our DO-ing. He knows the whole of us, and he shows us that we are his beloved ones, worthy of his mercy, his love, and his healing. He makes the gift of himself to us, not in spite of our weaknesses, but in part because of them. Our smallness calls to the greatness of his mercy.

A few years ago, my daughter Cecilia fell into a strange sleep-like state. She had had serious brain surgery the year before to try to stop the epileptic seizures that were becoming more and more frequent and dangerous. The surgery hadn't worked. When she began having the seizures again, she fell into hypersomnia, often getting up for only an hour a day. We didn't understand what was happening, at first. I would go into her room in the morning to wake her up for school, but she wouldn't get out of bed. She wasn't being disrespectful or disobedient. She just didn't feel able to get up. We went to several doctors, but no one had a solution. I tried a hundred different ways to coax her into getting out of bed. But they almost never worked. Day followed day. Weeks, and then months, went by. I felt like a complete failure as a mother. There was a great deal of "tension" in the house, a lot of shame, and guilt and blame. "You're letting her rot in her room! What kind of mother does that?!" That accusation fell into fertile ground. I was already filled with anguish and shame over not being able to get Ceci up. We were literally isolated. I almost never left the house, since I couldn't leave Ceci alone. I felt as though I was watching my daughter die inch by inch. I felt as if I was bleeding to death inside, powerless, defeated, guilty, and so ashamed.

Then early one morning, I read Mark's fifth chapter, and I knew! I knew I was the woman with the hemorrhage, isolated and bleeding. I was praying every day! But I was letting my own self-hatred and shame keep me from breaking out of my confinement. I knew I needed to "press forward" through all the voices of condemnation, the ones from outside and the ones inside, and I must reach out for the hem of his garment. I knew I had to persevere past the paralysis of the shame. I also knew that Jesus was upstairs next to my girl's bed, loving her and being with her. I heard him whisper in my anguished mother's heart, "Sally, your daughter is not 'dead.' She is only asleep." The crowds of my interior voices, never quiet, began shouting ridicule, speaking shame, telling me of my laziness, "revealing" to me how I "spoke" of his word and his power, but I did not "live" there! They were insistent, and almost deafening.

Jesus ordered them out. Then, in the quiet, alone with me, he leaned over, and taking my hand, with infinite tenderness, he whispered, "*Talitha kum*! Arise. Be healed. I bring life out of death. I will bring life out of this death you are living. I will bring life out of death for your sleeping daughter, our beloved girl." I felt as though I could take a breath for the first time in ten months.

Remember: "When God calls you, he empowers you." God never places a longing in our hearts and then deprives us of the grace to reach it. But we must say our *yes*. I had to stop telling myself I was a bad mother and start listening for his mercy and truth. "Arise, dear one!" When I did, I was able to arise. I made another appointment with another neuroendocrinologist. This time there was an answer. After watching my daughter "sleeping" for ten months, I watched her arise. I watched her get out of bed and walk around! I was astonished and overcome with gratitude and joy!

Sisters, do not let the voices, the ones from outside or the ones inside, tell you that you are not worthy. Read again what God has said in his holy Scripture. Read it over and over, until you can recite it to yourself, until God's words replace the words of shame, guilt, and condemnation. Write down the lies and find the Word of truth and love in Scripture, as Kristin does. *Know* that when God speaks, worlds are created! Say your *yes*, and let God speak the truth of your belovedness, the truth of your worthiness, and you will begin to live in his healing, peace, and freedom. Let him speak his love into you, and be created again as the exquisite, priceless, valuable woman you already are! ▪

saying yes to
CALLING

KRISTIN

The idea of our calling in life ties into one of the biggest questions of our existence—after the question "Who am I?" comes the question, "What was I created for?" These are huge, epic questions, and we grapple with them throughout many seasons of our lives. Whenever I speak or teach on this subject, many women respond to the question of calling with, "My calling is to be a wife. My calling is to be a mother."

These are high and noble roles, I agree, some of the hardest and most selfless efforts of a lifetime, but they are *roles*—not calling. There is a difference. Roles have to do with the way we define ourselves in terms of relationships, which we women absolutely love. But calling is something bigger than roles, more akin to identity than relationship or task. God crafted every single one of us for a specific purpose at a specific time in his divine plan. The question of calling is the unveiling of this assignment.

Ephesians 4:1 boldly instructs us to "live a life worthy of the calling you have received." The very idea of a calling can seem very daunting to most of us, because we are already struggling with feeling overwhelmed with just getting by. We also think about calling like it has to mean doing some huge thing—something new, notable, exceptional, and impressive. Or that our calling and our career are intertwined—they can be, but aren't always. I remem-

ber when my kids were little—a toddler and twin infants—
and I spent all day nursing or changing diapers, hoping for
a shower on an especially "productive" day. I remember
crying to my mom, exhausted and feeling futile in a new
baby haze, about what I was supposed to be *doing with my
life*. She responded with something that I never forgot and
have since shared with many women, one of my all-time
favorite Ethel-isms: "You can do everything, honey, just not
all at the same time." Calling is like that; it comes to us in
small steps and in seasons. Sally likes to say it is not some
giant *yes*, but more a series of small *yeses*.

Our calling originates in our creation. What I mean is,
our calling isn't really something we figure out as much
as we remember it or uncover it. Think about it this way:
What is something that you have always loved to do, ever
since you were a child? If you can't remember it's okay,
because you can always ask your mom, dad, sibling, or old
friend. What is the thing that used to make you lose track of
time, so immersed were you in your own enjoyment? What
is the thing that comes so naturally to you that you cannot
imagine that anyone would struggle with it? See, God created us to love what he created us to do. The fulfillment of
our calling is a mutual blessing—to us and to the world.

Frederick Buechner says it this way, "The place God
calls you to is the place where your deep gladness and the
world's deep hunger meet." The thing you absolutely love
to do, and are gifted to do, meets a need that serves others.
Finding our calling isn't something we stress or strive over;
it's more a following of our delight. Delight yourself in the

Lord and he will give you the desires of your heart (Psalm 37:4). One small *yes* after another. We focus on the process, doing the next right thing, and leave the outcome to God. He is building something incredible, bigger and more beautiful than we could ever imagine or understand. Think about the generations it took to build a cathedral—hundreds of years and the work of many hands over many lifetimes. If the cathedral is a metaphor for God's Kingdom, then we each have our work to do to build our part, during the assigned time we have here on earth. Each one of us has a contribution that is an essential and highly personal offering in the construction of the master plan. We have different gifts according to the grace given us (Rom 12:6).

These small *yeses* look different at different seasons in our lives. A student, a young single woman, a newlywed figuring out married life, a career woman, a mother of small children, an empty nester, a grandmother—all these seasons are different in terms of available time and energy. When we look to God for direction, it saves us from comparing, complacency, and criticism. God speaks clarity, not confusion. He will not ask us to do or be something that contradicts his word or instruction in another area. God is consistent and constant. And thank God, because we humans are simply not either of those things. We are prone to following whims and ego, posing the wrong questions at the wrong time, to the wrong people.

If we think that God is calling us to do something that compromises our values or our already established priorities, we need to pause and ask again. God will not ask us to do something that will sacrifice our marriage, our mothering, our presence, or our health. He isn't like that. He might ask us to do something challenging, but if he does, he will equip us to meet the challenge *and* maintain a balanced life. He is the God of Sabbath, after all. John 21 illustrates this phenomenon perfectly. The disciples are fishing, and having a rather lame go of it too. Jesus asks them how it's going and when they say it really isn't, he tells them to cast their nets on the right side of the boat. I imagine that they might have sighed and said an exasperated, eye-rolling "fiiiiine," the way my kids do when I tell them to look again, because I know right where they left the thing they are looking for. The disciples dropped their nets on the right side of the boat, and "were not able to pull it in because of the number of fish" (v. 6). There were one hundred fifty-three large fish in that net! But here's my favorite part, are you ready for this?

> Even though there were so many,
> the net was not torn. (v. 11)

The net was not torn!

Do you see? God's abundance, his instruction, his asking for our *yes*, his call on our lives, will not tear our nets. If he asks or instructs, he will equip both for the task itself *and* for the haul or harvest it yields.

If we are doing something, no matter how important we think it is or how important we think we are because we're doing it, and *our nets are tearing*, that is not God's doing; it's ours. Our calling energizes and delights us because it is what we were made to do with joy and ease and flow. Our calling will not stress us out, sacrifice our good health, exhaust and deplete us, or damage or neglect our relationships; it won't diminish our parenting effort or intentions; it won't blur our focus or obscure the God-given priorities of our hearts. On my own, I might tear my nets, trying to haul in too much out of my own striving, ego, or lack of balance. But God's way allows us to serve and not run empty, to bless and have more blessing flowing in.

What have you always loved to do? What comes easily and naturally for you? Where does this offering meet the world's need?

The intersection of offering and need, the sweet spot where passion and purpose collide, creates your Calling.

Say *yes.*

SALLY

B
eing able to say *yes* to our calling, means opening ourselves up to the truth of who we are: exquisite daughters of God. God formed each one of us in his own "image and likeness" (Genesis 1:27). But for each of us, the little piece of his image he planted in us was different: no two of them the same. As St. Paul says, in Romans 12:4–6, "Just as each of our bodies have several parts and each part has a separate function, so all of us in union with Christ, form one body, and as parts of it, we belong to each other. Our gifts differ according to the grace given to us." This means that in order to be the woman you are called to be, you just have to be yourself! There is no "Christian woman form" we are all supposed to squeeze into, which is a tremendous relief, given the way that form is mostly presented: always "en route" with a casserole for a sick someone, with three rosaries in your purse, wearing a serviceable denim dress with lots of embroidery that screams, "I do crafts!" Mind you, I love doing crafts, but I don't necessarily want to look like I do. To be truthful, I do make a lot of soup, and I know I have a couple of rosaries in my purse, which is actually a backpack, because of all the books I'm always dragging around. The point is, there is no "form" we have to follow. We just have to be ourselves.

The saints are, of course, a great example to us of what it looks like to give yourself entirely to God. But sometimes, they can be an obstacle too. We look at them, and don't you think, "there's no way I'll ever get there!" Shoot! I know myself. I know that when those accursed (kidding!) darling Girl Scouts stand outside the Walgreens with their cookies (it feels like a mortal sin to pass by their sweet, little hopeful faces. Oy!), I'll buy four or five boxes. When I get home, I'll open the Thin Mints box and say, "I'll just have two." Half a sleeve later, I remember that I'm a miserably weak woman when it comes to Thin Mints. If I can't keep myself from eating fifteen Thin Mints, how am I going to overcome my really significant weaknesses in order be conformed to Christ, and become a saint? Plus, I don't know if you've noticed, but the saints tended to die badly...and early. They also tended to do *big* things—start worldwide missions by picking up dying people or take the place of a condemned man in a concentration camp.... I'm a housewife, with six kids and three dogs, who lives in suburbia and drives an ugly, olive green Kia van. It's not really the "saint image" we have colored in and hanging on our refrigerators.

Ready for the good news? Here it is. Every single saint who ever lived, no matter what they did, or how seemingly inaccessibly holy they were, had one thing in common— and this one thing is what made them a saint. Every one of them fell in love and then followed their Beloved into holiness. How did they do that? They discovered what the little piece of his "image and likeness" looked like in them, and they figured out that being faithful to that piece of themselves *was* being faithful to God! Each one of us is called into holiness, because each of us was made by Love, for love's sake. Holiness is just what love looks like on the outside. Holiness is the piece of his "image and likeness" that looks just like you!

Looking at the lives of the saints, we are told to "imitate them." That's perfectly reasonable, of course, but sometimes I think that can throw us off too. We fashion an image of holiness for ourselves by looking at them, and thinking we are supposed to be "like them." I always loved St. Thérèse of Lisieux, and wanted to imitate her simplicity, courage, and joy. She was my confirmation saint. But as much as I have loved her, and read her, and tried to be like her, I also have felt tremendous discouragement, and even shame, at times, when I see how very much I'm *not* like her. Secretly, I thought God was having a really great day when he fashioned St. Thérèse. But the day he fashioned me, he had a bit of a headache, and he just did the best he could. This is where our trying too hard to imitate the saints can become a hindrance to us. Father Jacques Philippe says, "The greatest obstacle on the path of holiness may be to cling too closely to the image we have of our own perfection" (*In the School of the Holy Spirit*, p. 18). Father goes on to say that the best *we* can do is "imitate," but if we will listen for God's inspirations of grace (what do you love doing? What makes you feel full?), and follow them (him), he will create, with you, the unique masterpiece of your particular holiness.

It all begins with a *yes*. An angel appeared to Mary and said, "Hail, Full of grace, the Lord is with you." Mary said her *yes*. The Holy Spirit overshadowed her, and Christ was conceived in her, quietly growing in her for nine months. Then, Love was born into the world, the Incarnation of God. Mary's faith, and her love, gave her the courage to say *yes*, and then the Holy Spirit planted Love in her womb. Every call from God is a call to life!

Here, we pay attention. Faith precedes conception. First, she believed; then she conceived. To discover and live in our calling, is our own "annunciation," our *yes* to the grace we find in front of us. Our *yes* allows the conception of the calling he planted in us. The *yes* quietly grows in us. *Yes* follows upon *yes*: little annunciations that lead to the birth of love, to the discovery and joy of "giving flesh" to our calling. Like Mary, we won't be told the "end of the story" at the beginning. Mary woke up every morning in the excitement of the discovery of what her *yes* was going to mean that day. We won't know the fullness of our calling or the true beauty and power of its "incarnation" for a long, long time—maybe, not until we stand in his arms in heaven. Still, we will have lived our annunciation, and he will have been born into the world through us.

George Bernard Shaw said, "Life isn't about discovering yourself. It's about creating yourself." That's mostly true. There is some discovery required—recognizing your capacities, gifts, passion, curiosity, abilities, and desires, all of which compose the unique piece of his image and likeness given to you in trust, and with love, at your conception. That piece is about believing. The rest is about conceiving. Saying *yes* to God, and to the truth of yourself, and then deciding together what the "incarnation" of your calling will look like in the world. We won't know the end of the story when we say the *yes* of this day, or the *yes* of tomorrow. But its incarnation will grow in us with every decision we make, every *yes* we say to what we meet each day. It's also helpful to know that even when we feel too weak or over-whelmed and all we can say is "no," the Beloved will just find another way to offer us that grace. Sometimes, the *yes* we say after a *no* is even more beautiful than the original *yes* would have been. So don't beat yourself up when you feel like you haven't responded out of the truth of yourself and in faithfulness to Love. He'll just walk around and find a window he can slip through. He is the most persistent lover in the universe.

Knowing yourself, moving in the direction your long-ing, talent, curiosity, and ability seem to draw you toward, is one way to discern your calling. The other is to be pres-ent where you are and look at what is in front of you in your life, your work, and your relationships. Calling is always embedded in the truth of what we meet every day. Discernment of our calling is often about just responding with as much love, faithfulness, truthfulness, courage, and mercy to what's right in front of you. Calling is a progres-sive revelation. It's almost never a burning bush that speaks to you on the way out the door to the grocery store. Even a calling that seems clear is often only clear in the beginning. This is why prayer, the sacraments, and Holy Scripture are essential to both discerning our call and to living it out. They help us to refine the calling.

As you move more deeply into it, the Beloved draws you

down paths we did not know we would be asked to walk. We often worry that we won't be "equipped" for what we can't anticipate. But the Beloved does not tell us in advance what he will place before us, because then we are inclined to be self-sufficient, and we want control. So he hides from us so that we will seek him and encounter our great need for his grace. Then, we must remember: if God calls you, he empowers you. He would never plant in you a deep longing and then deprive you of the grace to accomplish it. When you are trying to live out your calling, and things get really hard, as they will, just remember, "God calls me, and he empowers me!" This is important, because some aspects of living out our calling will seem beyond us; and without his grace, they are.

Some years ago, I had taught a class, and afterward a lovely woman came up and said, "I just don't want to end up being a burden to my children." I was quiet and then said, "I hope I'm a burden to mine!" I know that sounds terrible, like I'm trying to get revenge on them for all the trouble they caused me. But they weren't much trouble, and in any case, I didn't mean that at all. I went to pick up my kids from my mother's house, and she and I ended up having a long conversation about what the woman had said. Let's be honest, no one wants to end up infirm, and incapacitated. But what if the Beloved said, "Will you offer me one last gift? Will you let me use your infirmity so that your children may be given the gift of having to learn to love outside of themselves? Will you let me break down the edges of what is comfortable, so that they can love the way I love…all the way to the cross?" Mother and I tried to be brave, and so together we said our little *yes* in Mother's living room, which for that moment, was our "garden of the annunciation."

Two years ago, when she was eighty-two years old, my mother had a fall. She had begun having some loss of memory and some confusion in the year before, but the fall threw her into full-blown dementia. Mother had been vibrant, bright, energetic, generous, courageous, full of love, and weaknesses too. She had started programs for underprivileged kids and had taken care of every person who stepped into her house. Her calling evolved and grew and went places she never could have guessed. But she always said *yes* with everything she had! She drove around in a red VW bug convertible and never stayed in her own lane—but no one seemed to mind. She would just wave and they'd always wave back. She went to Mass every day, and said the Rosary. She helped anyone who needed help but also had no sense of boundaries, which made her periodically very difficult to manage. My brothers and sisters and I used to say, "If it's not one thing, it's your mother!"

It was heartbreaking to see this "alive," sparkling woman become old, frail, and afraid. My brothers and sisters and I, and some of the older grandchildren, took turns taking care of her, because in her confusion and weakness she could not be left alone. She needed help getting up, going to the bathroom, dressing herself. She developed diabetes, and her blood sugar had to be monitored. But she couldn't really taste anything anymore, so it was hard to get her to eat. I still took her to Sunday Mass, but it was almost always an ordeal, a three-hour marathon of dressing, transporting, being in Mass (right in the front, on the Mary side), and then all of that in reverse. Mother, who had been a tall, elegant, woman who had modeled for Chanel and Dior in Paris, became bones and skin—eighty-seven pounds.

But planted in the middle of her dementia, she would have times when she was almost completely lucid. Those were times of grace and of suffering. She would cry, "Sally! Why is God letting this happen? I thought I was still useful to him! I don't understand why my mind is leaving me. Why won't anyone help me?" Oh my gosh! She was suffering so much. It makes me cry to think of it. But it was also a time of grace. I would tell her, "Mama. Don't you remember our prayer? You said you wanted to give Jesus one last gift; you wanted to help him teach us how to love like he does. Now, that's what you're giving him! It's your most beautiful gift to him, ever!" Sometimes, she would remember, and then she would quiet, and a sweet smile would light up her face. Other times, she didn't, and I would just have to start telling her about something funny one of the kids had done, or sing to her. Mostly, I would just lie down next to her and hold her hand. Each one of us had to meet those moments. Each of us had to take our very modest mother to the bathroom. Each of us had to devise ways for her to eat. Each of us had to find ways to quiet her when she was afraid.

She and I went to her last Mass on the Assumption of the Blessed Virgin Mary. A week later, she died, with almost all of her children and grandchildren around her. I was kneeling at her feet, praying Psalm 63:

O God, you are my God, for you I long,
My soul is thirsting for you,
My flesh is longing for you, like a dry and waterless land;
I long to gaze on you in your sanctuary,
To see you in your holy place.

Your love is better than life,
My lips will sing your praise,
All my life I will bless you,
In your name I lift up my hands;
My soul will feast and be glad,
My lips will sing a song of joy, and my mouth, praise.

On my bed I think of you,
I meditate on you all night long,
For you have always helped me.
I will sing for joy in the shadow of your wings;
My soul clings to you,
And your right hand holds me up.

As I came to this last verse, Mama took her last breath. She had fulfilled her calling. She had made her last, and maybe her most beautiful, gift. She had given birth to all of us, and in the last year of her life she helped give birth to us again. For at the end of that year, none of us were the same. Each one of us in our own way had received the gift the Beloved was giving us through her offering and had learned to love much past the edges of our own smallness. She was a mother to us until the very end. Saying her *yes* to this suffering, she opened a way for us to learn to say *yes* to our calling—the very great calling of learning to love the way Jesus does, all the way to the end.

We all hold in ourselves a great calling. It is one that has never been lived before, a masterpiece God will make with us, and in us. If we press into the heart of our self, we can discover what the first glimmering light of it might be. Say *yes* to that truth in you, and believe that God held that priceless piece of himself until it was time to reveal it in the particular beauty of your unique calling. Saying *yes* to him, is saying *yes* to our true self. It is saying *yes* to fulfillment and joy. It is our participation in the annunciation, our *yes* that gives birth to Love in the world. And dearest, the world will never be the same! *You* will shine with your own perfectly beautiful and unique piece of his image and likeness. This never-before-seen piece of him will have been born into the world through you. Your calling will meet a need the world doesn't yet know it longs for. Your joy and the world's need will collide, and you will be living in the indescribable goodness and gift of your calling. All it takes is the first little *yes*. The rest will follow as you wake each day in the excitement of the discovery of what your *yes* is going to look like today! ▪

CHAPTER 3

saying yes to

IMPERFECTION

KRISTIN

For many years I said *yes* to being perfect.

The world told me to make good grades, so I made A's. The world told me to be thin, so I ate less. The world told me to go to college and get a job and stay the path, so I did the next thing in front of me, never considering if it was what I wanted to do, what I should be doing, what I was created and gifted and ordained and assigned to do. I thought I should be a perfect wife, so I never questioned or argued. In my quest to be a perfect teammate, I completely lost myself before I ever lost my marriage. I thought I had to be the perfect mother, especially after my divorce, so I showed up and signed up for everything. If I could have torn myself apart and cloned three mommies, one for each of my children, I would have, so as not to miss a single moment.

My *yes* to perfection eliminated my prospects of being *good enough* or having a life that was *good enough*. I wore myself down to a nub, a shell, a brittle and narrow version of a formerly strong and vast person.

One of my favorite stories about imperfection is from Luke 2:41–52. Mary is pretty much the perfect mother, right? After all she was chosen by God himself to bear and raise his only Son. In this passage we get to hear a family vacation story from Jesus' childhood. He was twelve years old at the time, so likely an eye-rolling adolescent if he even eye-rolled. (My kids certainly do.) They were coming back from a family trip to Jerusalem for the Passover feast, and Mary and Joseph could not locate Jesus in the caravan. In classic *Home Alone* fashion, unbeknownst to his parents, Jesus had stayed behind in the temple in Jerusalem. After Jesus was MIA for a day, they started searching for him and couldn't find him, so they retraced their steps back to Jerusalem, where they finally found their preteen son *three days later*, sitting in the temple.

Let's think about this for a second. Losing your kid for four days? I lost Luke once in a department store for about ten minutes; the little stinker was hiding in the middle of a clothes rack laughing while I sobbed and hollered his name. I lost my daughter Grace at a local kite festival for about five minutes, and I was sick and shaky. In my mind I saw myself printing MISSING flyers and holding a press conference on CNN. Mary lost Jesus for four days. *Four days* to have misplaced the Son of God! Can you *imagine* how she felt? Can you imagine the sick shock of mother anguish for a lost son combined with a healthy fear of God, who also happens to be his *Father*? I shudder to imagine. I wonder if she and Joseph argued, "I thought you were watching him!" I plan to ask Mary about this when I get to heaven. And also thank her for allowing this story to make the baby book. Why? Because knowing that Mary wasn't perfectly perfect really helps me accept my parenting moments when I am not perfectly perfect either.

Becoming okay with our imperfections, saying *yes* to them with awareness and grace, requires vulnerability.

Viewed through a lens of perfection, vulnerability looks a lot like weakness. Viewed through a lens of faith, vulnerability looks like the catalyst to strength.

In 2 Corinthians 12:9, the Lord says to St. Paul: "My grace is sufficient for you, for my strength is made perfect in weakness."

In this sense, our imperfections are not a wall between us and God, but a doorway. Our weaknesses are the very things that continuously draw us back to God. And they are things that pull God's power into us. Our imperfections are the path to vulnerability, which is the path to intimacy. Intimacy with God. Intimacy with our true selves. And intimacy with each other.

Think of some women you know who present this veneer of perfection. I'm not casting stones; I used to do this. It was my defense mechanism to keep people at arm's length so they couldn't really see me, up close, when my life was messy. We see these women, perfectly put together, dressed and poised and in control. Or so we think. When I was going through my divorce and my kids were 3, 1, and 1, it soon became impossible to manage my misery and appear perfectly put together.

The preschool where my kids went had a drop-off line filled with fresh, dressed, nicely made-up mommies with lattes in the cup holders of their SUVs. They dropped off clean children dressed in khakis and collared shirts, or Mary Janes and big bows clipped to nicely combed bob haircuts. I gave up trying to fit in. I had to.

I careened in at the tail end of the drop-off line, wearing

pajamas with bed-head hair and a sloshing cup of lukewarm coffee between my legs in a crooked handmade cup made by my kids at a ceramics place. My girls wore only Target tulle princess dresses and rubber frog rain boots. Luke liked to wear a bike helmet, all the time. They ate toaster waffle strips on paper plates in their car seats on the way to school, rubbing syrup hands in their uncombed hair. We were feral. Ah, I miss those days.

I am reminded of *The Velveteen Rabbit*. I love that story. The stuffed rabbit is well worn, with nubby fur and a missing boot-button eye—and he becomes real, *because he was loved*. Over time, imperfection starts to look real. Then it starts to look an awful lot like love.

When we start to present our imperfect real self to other women is precisely the time we start to have real friends— the kind who walk in when the world walks out; the ones who know when to show up, when to shut up, and when to speak up. When we start to show our imperfect self to our husbands is when our marriages start to get real. When we are finally courageous enough to show our softness is when men can bring us their strength. When we let our children see our imperfection they can begin to love us as authentic people—as women and as mothers. When we can look at our kids and say, "I really don't like how I handled that. Can I have a do-over? This is what I wish I said instead…" When we allow God access to our brokenness, our mess, our ugliness, and our shortcomings is precisely when we start cooperating with him in our healing. God already knows all our flaws; after all he created us. He just wants to know that *we* know them. He wants to know that we know that he is God and we are not. Humility is the catalyst to unprecedented transformation. A perfect person isn't aware that they have any need for God, or any work to do at all. An imperfect woman knows that she is already good enough, but that God loves her too much to leave her that way.

I have dear friends in Spain—a college friend of mine married a woman I adore, and they are my daughters' god-parents. They live in Barcelona. We went to visit them and after a long Spanish night with cava and conversation, I told them how I wanted to fall in love again—but I never met anyone perfect.

Ana looked at me with her wise brown eyes and said, "I wish for you, *un hombre imperfecto que te quiera en una manera perfecta*." An imperfect man who loves you in a perfect way.

My heart melted. I decided to hold out for him, for as long as it took.

Let us be open to seeing ourselves in a mirror that reflects us the way God sees us. Not the scary 7x magnifying mirror like I have in my bathroom that brutally reflects every crinkle, every spot, and even the occasional scary rogue chin hair. No. I mean the mirror that shows us our beauty, our greatness, our potential, our identity, our security, and our worth. Our gloriously imperfect perfection.

Those who look to him are radiant. *Psalm 34:5*

SALLY

Kristin offers us a new place to stand—a place where we are seen and known and loved for who we are. This means letting ourselves be loved as we are right this minute, not for who we might become when, or if, we finally "get it together." This is one of the great secrets of the spiritual life: if we let him, God will use our imperfections, the very things we think are the most unlovable about ourselves, to show us how deeply, and utterly, we are loved. Our imperfection becomes the door his mercy rushes through.

St. Thérèse of Lisieux, in a letter to a friend, tried to explain what this kind of love looks like. She tells the story of two children on a rainy day. Their father is at home, down the hall in his study. The kids start playing with a ball in the living room. They know they're not supposed to, but they're bored and they can't go outside because of the rain. Sure enough, the ball careens off a table and breaks the window. The first child runs upstairs to hide in his room. He's afraid of his father's anger and his judgment. The second child bolts down the hall, throws open the door of her father's study, launches herself into his lap, and says, "Kiss me, and tell me that you love me!" The father kisses her and says, "I love you, dearest."

Then she tells him about the window.

In our own experience, this would be the part where the

father looks at her sternly and says, "Didn't I tell you not the play with the ball inside?" But this is the moment that Thérèse reveals the breathtaking truth of the father's love. She tells us that the father gathers his daughter up, pressing her closer to his heart, and kisses her even more tenderly. The father's heart is deeply touched by her confidence in his love. She ran to him in her weakness and let him gather her up. She trusted him with her smallness, and his heart is taken captive. She was loved into life!

So much of the time, we are like the first child. We stumble, and we think God must be disappointed in us. So we run away and try to hide behind our carefully constructed "veneer of our perfection." But it's not the *stumble* that wounds love. It's the *running*. The running means we don't trust his love for us. The running means we believe in a demanding, judgmental, petty God—and that's not who he is at all. He is immense and beautiful. He loves us so deeply and unconditionally. He longs for us to trust him with our weakness. Would the little girl have known how deeply the father loved her, if she hadn't stumbled? How can any of us experience the power of God's love if we haven't had to acknowledge our tremendous need for it?

I would never have known how much I needed the Beloved if I hadn't come face to face with my imperfection. I had loved him for as long as I can remember, and I had pursued him in my heart and in my work. As I was having many babies (I'm a nice Catholic girl, after all!), I slowly took classes in theology. I had just had baby number five and was in the middle of my second Masters in theology when the Beloved gave me the great gift of seeing myself as I truly was, not as I believed myself to be, and certainly not as I was presenting myself to the world. Sometimes his gifts come wrapped in circumstances that look nothing like we would ever want. They come wrapped in grief and in a darkness so complete, we can't even see the hand in front of our face. But whether or not we recognize it as a gift, it still is. St. Teresa of Ávila, during one of those dark moments, said, "Jesus was holding me so close to his heart, that I could not see his face." I came to see that whenever God hands us something painful and difficult with one hand, he always hands us mercy with the other. But his mercy almost never comes in shiny, obvious paper—it comes in the plain paper that looks just like our ordinary life.

The Beloved began to draw me closer to his heart through my brilliant and wonderful husband, Brad. (We shouldn't be surprised how often the Beloved uses our spouses to call us more deeply into himself; though we often are.) From the outside, our family looked like a normal, happy family. Brad was very successful in his work. The children were bright, did well in school, and were a joy to be around. I was being a diligent mom and getting graduate degrees. We seemed to have it all together. But inside, we were falling apart. Brad was in the grip of a terrible and murderous disease—alcoholism. He is a gentle, kind man, so he never raged or yelled at us, which made the recognition harder, in some ways. Late-stage alcoholics teach us to look at the wrong things. We think an alcoholic gets sloppy, yells, loses his job, passes out. Some do. But many go to work and seem pretty together, though there are always "signs." Brad was one of the functional ones. He was a successful executive by day, but then he would come home and "disappear." I know that it could have been so much worse, but it was immensely painful for all of us. I needed my husband. The children needed their father. And Brad needed to be healed.

I would get up early in the morning and pray like crazy, hours and hours on my knees, asking for God to heal Brad. He was, after all, the one with "the problem." The Beloved answered me in a way I never expected. He always moves in love when we pray, but he answers the deepest prayers, the ones we haven't put words to yet. His answer to my unceasing prayer was to show me myself. You see, I knew alcoholism was a disease. In the beginning, it is willful. But at some ill-defined time in the middle, it becomes something that grabs a person by the throat and "takes them where they do not want to go." I knew that's where Brad was, but I was furious at him, anyway. We were all hurting so much, and he kept drinking. My anger wasn't logical; it was visceral. Because I was a "nice Christian woman," I wasn't openly angry. I didn't turn into the snarling, witchy wife. What I did was worse. I stayed busy. I had five kids, so there was lots to do—peanut butter and jelly sandwiches to make, teachers to meet with, practices to drive to, school projects that needed to be done....No one drinks because they are happy and at peace. They drink because they are hurting beyond knowing what to do. So they try to quiet the voice inside that fills them with regret, anguish, and shame, the one that tells them every minute of the day that they're "not worth loving."

I left Brad alone in his darkness. He was turning to dust inside, and I was not there to tell him how infinitely dear he was to me. I was mad. So I stayed busy, doing all the millions of things that had to get done. And I did something else. I made myself the "hero" of the story—"the heroic martyr," doing everything to hold the family together. Mind you, everything I did needed to be done. But it should have been done as a gift, not as a "martyr saint." Martyr saints of that kind don't produce holiness. They just generate more shame—something Brad didn't need any more of.

As long as I was playing the role of "perfect hero/martyr," I could not see myself as I was. Loving me, God stepped through the door I had opened with my prayer. With careful but relentless mercy, he cracked open the veneer of my perfection and let me see my grievous imperfections. I saw that I was selfish, resentful, self-righteous, and full of fear. I was ashamed and heartbroken to see myself without the protective, comfortable veneer I had so carefully fashioned. Though my faith had been very sincere up to that time, this was a time of deep conversion. A time of turning toward the truth and discovering Love. Seeing myself as I truly was, I came to understand, in a way I had never understood before, how much I needed Jesus as my Savior!

Whenever God hands you something difficult with one hand, he hands you mercy with the other. The mercy in the other hand came in a reading I stumbled across. I was reading a book written by a mystic who believed Jesus came and spoke to her about his daily life. Honestly, I don't know if he really spoke to her or not. What I do know is that the short passage I read was true, true in the deepest sense. I heard his "voice" in these words, and I knew that he "spoke" them in the truth of the sacrifice of his love. The mystic asked Jesus what he was thinking about in the Garden of Gesthemane, at the beginning of his Passion. He said:

> Your name. Your name I whispered over and over
> to myself. Your name was like medicine instilled
> into my veins to make them function. Your name
> was for me light coming back, life coming back,
> strength coming back. When I thought the tortures
> were too great I whispered your name to myself so
> that I would have the strength to die. Since then,
> I saw you. Since then, I carried you in my heart.
> And when it was time to come onto the earth,
> I leaned out of heaven to accompany your coming,
> rejoicing at the thought that YOU were finally
> being born into the world. O! My blessed ones!
> The comfort of the dying Christ! As I hung upon
> the cross, I saw in front of me my mother, the
> beloved disciple and the pious women. But I also
> saw you. And my eyes closed thus, happy to be
> closed because they had saved you.

How could I ever be the same? Jesus did not die for "all mankind"—he died for *me*. He died for you too, as if no one else ever existed. He whispered my name so he would have the strength to die. He whispered your name, over and over to himself, holding you in his heart, rejoicing that his death would save you. How can any of us be the same? The only way to respond to such a gift is with our whole selves. With gratitude shot through every moment, with love that illuminates every darkness, with joy that makes us feel like we're splitting open and shooting sparks! My imperfections, my brokenness, became the door his mercy rushed through. He rolled away the stone from the tomb of my constructed self, and led me into healing, into joy, into resurrection, into life.

That would have been more than I could have asked or imagined, but the mercy he brought in his other hand was as immense as he is. Just before Christmas of last year, Brad celebrated his nineteenth year of sobriety. One day at a time, we watched my beautiful, courageous husband step into his sobriety with hard work, faithfulness, generosity, humility, and love. The mercy God brought to our hurting family is too big to try to squeeze into the small space words can define.

Allowing God access to our imperfection is the moment our healing begins. It's the moment we stop rationalizing and justifying, and we're quiet long enough to hear his deep, unconditional words of love to us. We're afraid of being broken, but we shouldn't be. It's not something that's *going* to happen to us at some awful time in the future. We're already broken. We've just finally recognized the fissures that are already there, and stopped trying to call them something else.

The questions God whispers to us are, "Beloved, will you trust me with your littleness? Will you give me your imperfections, your weakness, your selfishness, your ugliness? Will you let me squeeze in through the fissures in your broken heart?" He longs to enter through our brokenness, because it is there that we finally begin to understand how unspeakably beautiful we are to him. It's through the fissures of our imperfections that we can begin to let ourselves be loved into life, a life that splits open and shoots sparks— sparks that can set other hearts on fire. We will live every day, the glorious imperfect perfection! ▪

saying yes to
QUIET

KRISTIN

And Mary kept all these things, reflecting
on them in her heart. *Luke 2:19*

Rising very early before dawn, he left and went off
to a deserted place, where he prayed. *Mark 1:35*

Our culture today is an assault on quiet. Our
restlessness destroys our reverence. Our busyness frays our focus. The noise of life, pace,
screens, social media, news feeds, calendars,
and expectations all inhibit us from living the life we were
meant to live in Christ. Busy is one word I truly cannot
stand. In fact, my friends know I refer to it as the official "B"
bad word. We use the word "busy" as a panacea, an excuse,
a rationalization, a half-hearted apology, and a method to
self-promote. "Sorry, I am so busy!" "I have so much going
on you wouldn't believe it!" "Sorry I can't come, but I have
(insert litany of entire schedule)." Some of the most incredible, successful, impactful people I know never say they are
busy. Somehow they are running companies and raising
children and nurturing marriages and serving in ministry
and yet they always seem to have time to listen and be present. And then there are people doing a tiny fraction of all
this, who are "too busy" to connect, serve, seek, or make

any lasting impact at all. This was a mystery to me. Until I looked deeper, where the mysteries always originate.

In the above verse from Mark, we see how Jesus starts his day. He goes off to a quiet place to be alone and pray. If the Son of God needs his daily quiet time, do you think perhaps we might also? Jesus needed to connect to his Father. So do we. We should pay close attention not only to the fact that Jesus had this prayer practice but also *when* he had it. He got up early and connected to God first thing in the morning. Not everyone is a morning person; I know we are all wired differently this way. But we can all set our alarms ten to fifteen minutes earlier to set aside some time for quiet.

When we start the day without God, it often looks like this. The alarm blares, we hit snooze several times, and then finally catapult out of bed. We rush through the shower, throw on clothes, slam some coffee, hustle to the car, and hit rush hour traffic. Maybe we drop the kids late to school, squealing in on two wheels through the drop-off line, and then race into work late after the boss has already seen our empty desk. We seem to spend the whole day starting from behind, always trying to catch up, never able to get it all done. We pick up food on the way home because we didn't have time to get groceries, and we eat standing up in the kitchen, staring at our phones or catching up on emails we didn't get to at the office. The pile of unfolded laundry covers the sofa. Dishes collect in the sink. We collapse into bed exhausted; and the alarm blares the next morning, and we do it all again. And again and again, until all these days blur together and become the life we said we never wanted—a life devoid of reverence, reflection, connection, rest, passion, meaning, and intimacy.

When we are starved of quiet, an interesting thing happens. We forget we need it. We become afraid of it, what it might stir up, and what we might have to acknowledge about ourselves, our lives, or our relationships. We know we are in this place when see that we fill every opportunity for quiet with distraction. If we have ten minutes between scheduled blocks we fill it by checking our text messages, looking at email or Facebook, or making phone calls—anything to fill the void. Because when we are starved, quiet feels a lot like emptiness.

Sally says that quiet is not empty. She says quiet is where fullness begins. I love this thought. Quiet is the doorway into the sanctuary within each of us, the place where the Divine resides. The sanctuary is hard to get to at first, so we have to practice it by intentionally going there and spending time each morning, making ourselves at home. Over time we wear a familiar pathway to the sanctuary and can access it quickly, ducking in whenever a moment presents itself throughout the day. Our initial exploration of quiet becomes a daily devotion, a practice, a way of life. We have a place to recenter ourselves, to connect to God and his limitless supply of peace and presence. We can go there to quickly adjust our priorities and align our will with God's. Peace isn't something we are meant to long for later, when things slow down. They will never slow down. If we can't learn to find it now, we likely won't ever find it. Many of the things that keep us so frantic and busy are things that will never truly be "done." Quiet is not a luxury reserved for someday. Just like Sabbath is not just a day called Sunday. We were created to need God, and our soul runs dry when we deprive ourselves of quiet—because quiet is the pathway to him.

The time is now to create a quiet practice. Say *yes* to opening the doorway to your inner sanctuary. Set the alarm a bit earlier and find your way to connect to God, our Source of infinite energy, creativity, peace, joy, compassion, and love. A daily practice of prayer, Scripture reading, meditation, journaling, gratitude, or contemplation is essential to our spiritual well-being. We resist, saying we are too busy or don't have time, but try it for thirty days and you will see that spending time with God *creates* time. Quiet is a necessity, not a luxury. Find pockets of your day to fill with silence. Drive without the radio on or without calling someone on Bluetooth. Walk or run without headphones. Take a bath. Steal moments back from busyness. Reclaim reverence from rushing. I have a friend who sets an alarm reminder on her phone to ping her several times throughout the day and remind her to pause and breathe deeply. She says this small thing has changed her life. Luke 2:19 says that Mary reflected on things in her heart. When we are moving too fast or are distracted by all the noise, there is no space for reflection. There is no possibility of being present. We cultivate no awareness of gratitude. We have no capacity for intimacy or connection. We miss it all.

Peace is not waiting for the day when our lives slow down. God is Peace. And he is waiting for us right now, in the quiet. *Shhhhhhhhhhhhhhhhhhhhh.*

SALLY

Be still and know that I am God. *Psalm 46:10*

Did you know that God speaks not just to prophets, or hermits, or small energetic nuns picking leprous people off the streets of Calcutta, but to us? The Father whispers, "This is my beloved daughter in whom I am well pleased." The Beloved, the Son, the Word of God, whispers to us, "I love you." The Holy Spirit "overshadows" us, but it's like a cloud dashing across the sun—the light shifts, and then it's the same again. Did we even notice? Every day, in a hundred different ways, God whispers to us. But he is not loud or imposing. If we are never quiet, we won't hear him, and we won't recognize the flickering of the Holy Spirit as he flashes through our lives.

Our lives are noisy. We get up in the morning, and we are already "behind." Our whole day is filled with "checking things off the list." We fall in bed at the end of an endless day of box-checking, exhausted. But still there is no peace because our minds are filled with all of the things we didn't check off, all the ways we will wake up "behind." Busyness is deafening, and it's a codependent bully, always demanding our attention and making us feel guilty if we turn away from it.

Our lives are very loud and, if we're willing to be truthful, we don't like the quiet. How do we know this? Because we fill every quiet space with distraction. If there are ten minutes when we are between "boxes," we check our phone, look at email, turn on the TV, listen to the radio, read a romance novel, call somebody, send out a "just saying hi" text. Anything to fill the quiet—*because it feels like emptiness.*

But quiet is not empty. *Quiet is where fullness begins.* Quiet is where we can hear the Father whisper, "This is my beloved daughter in whom I am well pleased." Stillness is the only way to feel Jesus' arms around us and the only way to see the flickering light of Living Love overshadowing us. If we are not quiet, we cannot hear. If we are not still, we cannot see. If we are not at peace, we will not feel Love's embrace.

God knows full well the requirements and demands of our lives. He is not asking us to throw over all of our responsibilities and become a contemplative hermit. (So few of us look good in coarse, brown burlap—and those sandals!) No, he knows all the minute details of what is in front of us every day. What he wants is for us to meet these demands with fullness and peace, not frantic and overwhelmed.

How can we do this? How is peace possible in the middle of "the million things"? Don't we secretly think that those two things—peace and "the million things"—are contradictory? That they simply can't coexist? I've got six children, one of whom is differently abled. Sometimes it feels as though I have so many things I have to do, I'm underwater. But I found out a while ago that, no matter how early I got up, or how efficient I tried to be, or how organized, I still couldn't manage everything. I could never get everything done, in part because lots of the things I do, like the Himalayan piles of laundry and the endless dishes, don't *stay* done. (Can we hear an "Amen!"?) But St. Paul tells us that we are meant to be "filled with the peace of God, which is so much greater than we can understand" (Philippians 4:7). Which is true, isn't it? It doesn't make a lick of sense; we can't "understand" how we can possibly be at peace in the middle of such tremendously busy lives. But he wouldn't say that it was his intention for us and then tell us, "Gosh! I'm so sorry. You're too busy. Peace isn't possible for you. You'll have to radically alter your life and then you might be able to squeeze some peace in around the edges." That would be kind of awful, wouldn't it? You couldn't get around the idea that God was almost sadistic. St. Thérèse of Lisieux was acutely aware of this problem. She explained that God would never show us a good—he would never permit us to desire a deeper love, or a greater closeness, or long for a more beautiful holiness—and then deprive us of the grace we need to bring it into the truth of our life. If we desire a good, he is there already in the desire, and he will be there for us in every step along the way toward it (though he often "refines" the good along the way, so it may not look like what we thought it would at the beginning).

So, let's throw caution to the wind and assume that God is not sadistic, that he has held out the promise of peace

with the intention that we are to live there. One of his
names in Holy Scripture is Prince of Peace (Isaiah 9:6). We
are called to live in him. He is our true home. And when
we are at home, we will be whole and full and joyful and at
peace. What good would it be if those things weren't possible in the middle of the life we are living? If somehow peace
was always somewhere else?! No, Jesus was quite explicit.
"Come to me, all you who are weary and burdened, and I
will give you rest [peace]. Take my yoke upon you and learn
from me, for I am gentle and humble of heart, and you will
find rest [peace] for your souls. For my yoke is easy and my
burden is light" (Matthew 11:28–30). Then, right before
he enters into his Passion, he says, "Peace I leave with you;
my own peace I give to you. It is a peace the world cannot
give, for it is a gift I give to you" (John 14:27). The peace
he gives is the door *joy* breaks through! "May the God of
hope fill you with all joy and peace as you trust in him, so
that you may overflow with hope by the power of the Holy
Spirit" (Romans 15:13).

Peace fills the home God has made for us, but the front
door we have to open to go in is *Quiet*. Without quiet, we
can't hear his whispered words of love. Without quiet, we
won't see him moving across our lives because we won't
be still long enough to notice him. Something will happen
(doesn't it always?)—a flat tire, a kid that comes down
with strep, a time in our marriage when we feel unseen
and unloved....you know: you can fill in your blanks—and
we'll think, "Oh no! Really, God? Why is this happening?"
Without quiet, we can't see his handprints on what comes to

us. When we are still enough to see his handprints, "we remember that he is God, and he does miraculous things" (Psalm 105:5), and we know that "all things work together for those who love him" (Romans 8:28). Knowing that, we can find peace.

Here's the biggest problem: "My life is so packed! I don't have time for prayer."

There is a wonderful, and absolutely true, story of a priest who didn't have the "time" to pray the Rosary. He was the pastor of a big church in Paris and his day was packed from the wee hours of the morning to late at night. At the end of his day, he would fall into bed exhausted, only to "hit the ground running" before morning's first light. But he was told by a holy, and very pushy nun that the Blessed Mother was asking him to pray her prayer of meditation every day. He patiently explained why that was simply not possible. She said, "Do it anyway." What do you do when a holy woman looks you in the eye and says, "Do it"?

Pinched between the proverbial rock and a hard place, he grudgingly began praying the Rosary when he woke up in the morning. At the end of the first week, he noticed that, surprisingly, he had a half hour of "free time" at the end of his day. He was pleased because it gave him time to do some of the reading he had wanted to do. By the end of the third week of praying the Rosary every day, he found that he had an *hour* of time. In two months, he had two hours! He tried to think of what had changed. He was mystified, because he was every bit as busy as he usually was. As he thought more, he realized that the *only* thing that had changed was that he had taken the time to pray the Rosary every day. With a shock of recognition, he knew—his *yes* to Our Mother's prayer of meditation had made a space for her to say *yes* to him. And because she is a mother, her *yes* to him was very practical. Every day, the meetings he had seemed to just go more smoothly. The time he had to spend taking care of the ancient church building was somehow spent more efficiently, even though the demands on his time were every bit as heavy as they had always been, and in some cases, even more so. But somehow, he had "found" two hours at the end of the day, and with great joy, he also found that he had more time to spend with the dear people given to him to care, which was the real reason he had become a priest in the first place. He came to see that the Blessed Mother was going in front of him, and standing beside him, and holding him up over the rough spots. She "created time." The "time" he thought he did not have to pray was given back to him many times over because she was going before him in everything he did. He discovered a great mystery, one of the miracles of prayer: *spending time creates time.*

With that knowledge, how can you afford *not* to pray?!

Three other things you need to know about prayer: Prayer is not a technique; it is a grace. If you desire to pray, then God is already handing you the grace you need to pray—you wouldn't even desire it if he hadn't planted the desire in you in the first place. The second thing is: there is no "method" of prayer that is more effective than another. The only truly effective method of prayer is the one that you'll do! Every single person will find their own way to pray; it will be in accordance with their own strengths and weaknesses. Third, what do you "need" to do? Just this: "When you pray, go into your room and shut the door and pray to your Father who is in secret; and your Father who sees in secret will reward you" (Matthew 6:6). And the last thing is something Fr. Philippe wrote in his book on prayer *Time for God*: "In prayer, it is not 'quality' that matters, it is fidelity. The prayer can seem 'poor,' but if it is regular and faithful, it will be infinitely valuable. It is faithfulness alone that enables the life of prayer to bear wonderful fruit" (*Time for God*, p. 17).

Finally, dear ones, remember, "Eye has not seen, and ear has not heard, nor the human heart conceived, what God has prepared for those who love him" (1 Corinthians 2:9).

Prayer is the source of all true happiness. Those who pray will find the Living Water, "Whoever drinks the water that I shall give [her] will never thirst" (John 4:14). That sounds like a pretty great way to meet every busy day! ▨

CHAPTER 5

saying yes to
NO

KRISTIN

When Jesus was an infant, Mary and Joseph took him to the temple for his presentation, in accordance with Jewish tradition. A devout man named Simeon was in the temple, and according to Scripture (Luke 2:25) the Holy Spirit was upon him. He had some pretty powerful blessings to proclaim over the baby Jesus. He said this baby boy would become a light for revelation to the Gentiles and a glory for the people of Israel. He said Jesus was destined for the rise and fall of many and that he would be a sign that would be contradicted. He concluded with a little zinger for Mary that would strike fear into the heart of any mother. A warning, stated almost as an afterthought: "and *you yourself a sword will pierce*" (v. 35).

It sounds rather ominous, yes? Mary had no idea just how accurate this would prove to be. No mother wants to watch her son be crucified. And yet it is impossible to get through motherhood, or to love at all for that matter, and emerge unscathed. To truly love (and truly live) is to open your heart so wide that it is vulnerable to being pierced.

This chapter is a hard one. It treads on some delicate territory. We will all be pierced. At some point, we will all be handed moments that we want to refuse. A sick or injured child. The death of a loved one. Divorce. Betrayal. Losing a job. I have seen glimpses of it in my own life, and I've watched beloved friends as their knees buckled under the weight of bad news. My friend whose husband had a heart attack and died during the ocean swim portion of a triathlon. Another friend whose son overdosed as a freshman in college. A friend with addiction and depression who took her own life and left three children behind. A friend whose husband died slowly of liver cancer, leaving her and three children without a father. These are not *yes* moments. These are *no*. Maybe even "Hell, no!"

No one in her right mind wants to experience suffering of this magnitude, or any magnitude. We live in a culture of such convenience and comfort that it's almost outrageous when we are thrown into discomfort, inconvenience, and suffering. We go into shock, alternating between denial, numbness, anger, and grief. We feel like a victim of circumstance or misfortune, or even a victim of a merciless and cruel God. We fall apart. We shut down. We shatter.

All these reactions are normal responses to trauma, pain, and loss.

There really is no "human" way to say *yes* to no. From the vantage point of desolation there is no way to see that what is happening to us is actually happening *for* us. It's not possible to fathom that from the eye of the storm. The best we can hope for in the midst of a storm is to find something to hold onto in the waves, to find a lighthouse on the shore so we have a beacon toward hope, and to wait for the waves to pass.

My friend Jena, who lost her husband in the triathlon, said the waves never stop, or at least they haven't for over four years now. They just get smaller and farther apart, with a chance to float for a bit in between. I believe her. Because I am close to Jena, I got to see her up close when her storm was raging. It is a profound honor to be a friend to someone in this place. I remember she came to our Bible study about a week after Ross died. No one expected to see her. She walked in and plopped on the sofa with us and we all sobbed. There. Are. No. Words. And then the most unforgettable thing happened, something that changed my faith journey as much as any personal experience. Jena started to pray, something like this…

"Lord, I have no idea what you are doing right
now. I'm so broken and so angry at you. Yet I have
nowhere to go but to you. Comfort me; save me.
Help me comfort my children during these unthink-
able times. I have no desire in me to thank you,
but I will. Thank you for being with us right now.
Thank you for picking up the pieces of our family
and putting us back together eventually. Thank you
for helping us sleep without nightmares and for
leading us in the direction of joy again somehow,
some way. Thank you for giving us hope for better
times. Thank you for giving me the strength to raise
these children by myself, with you. I don't understand you, or this, but I do know I love you and I
trust that you love us. Thank you for the big angel
that now watches over us. I pray in the name of
Jesus. Amen."

I cannot recount this without crying. I was leveled, floored, speechless. Here was a woman in the middle of wreckage, *thanking God*. She was somehow saying *yes* to No. I asked her about it recently, and she has no memory of the words she prayed that day.

I had my own *yes* to *no* moment in 2003. My marriage fell apart, for the second and final time; I knew it was done. There was nothing left to salvage. We were in Spain at the time, and I had no friends or family close by to run to. I had neglected my faith, and myself. I was utterly broken, spent.

I left our apartment and walked around the village where we lived, aimless and blurry-eyed with tears. I wandered around until I found myself at the base of a huge flight of steps, and I followed them into the cathedral. The stained glass in the darkness, the cool air within the ancient stone walls, the candles burning, the smell of old hymnals, the quiet—it was everything familiar when there was nothing familiar. I sat in a pew and wept and prayed for hours. I look back on that day and know that God called me home to him. When everything fell apart, I still remembered where to go for comfort. After years of ignoring him, I still recognized his voice. In my devastation and my mess, he was waiting for me. I remember thanking him for his patience, thanking him for taking care of me, Luke, Grace, and Isabelle. I returned to our apartment with an incomprehensible feeling of lightness and peace in the middle of my misery. I had new strength and the resolve to make a plan to pack up my family and fly us home.

The one thing we cannot, must not, do is compare

wreckage. It's tempting to do so. *Well, mine is worse. Or thank God, yours is worse.* Ultimately, it's all wreckage. It's all No.

I believe that there is no human way to say *yes* to no. There is only the path of Divine Love that leads to *yes*. We cannot access this level of yes through willpower or determination. They say that time heals everything, but I don't even think time is enough to get to *yes* in situations like these. I believe that there is a key, a way to shortcut the lesson, not to circumvent the pain or the journey, but a way to cooperate with God in our healing and the renovation of our new normal.

The key is gratitude.

I realize it seems incomprehensible to say thank you to God when we are broken and furious. But I can tell you it is possible; I've seen it done several times, and I've even done it myself. I hope I remember to do it next time a storm blows in. I try to do it when small things disappoint or frustrate me, practicing to change my default reaction in lesser moments to prepare for the epic ones. If we can practice gratitude, we can learn to claim God's presence and sovereignty right when we need him the most.

Gratitude is the catalyst to grace.

SALLY

There is a wonderful story of an exchange between a young disciple and a rabbi in Parker Palmer's book *The Politics of the Brokenhearted.* The disciple asks the rebbe, "Why does the Torah tell us to place these words UPON our heart? Why does it not tell us to place these holy words IN our hearts?" The rebbe answers, "It is because as we are, our hearts are closed, and we cannot place the holy words in our hearts. So we place them on top of our hearts. And there they stay until, one day, our hearts break, and the words fall in."

I've spent a lot of my life wandering around with "the words on top of my heart." Mind you, I didn't know that. I was doing the best I could, trying to be a good and thoughtful person, a loving wife, an engaged and joyful mother, a good sister and daughter and friend. I prayed and was sincere and diligent in my faith. I won't tell you that none of God's holy words had penetrated my being and my deepest heart, because I know they had. The goodness I lived was generated out of these words that had somehow made it "in," these words who, for us as Catholics, are the Word of God, Jesus, the Christ. I know that he was in me, and I was in him. Still, so many of the words sat on top of my heart. "The Lord is kind and merciful, slow to anger and deep in compassion" (Psalm 103:8). With great sincerity, I was sure I knew what those words meant. I believed them with all my heart. I just didn't know that I believed with only the outside layer. By the way, I don't, at least anymore, fault myself for being as I was—young, confident, sure of myself, my faith, and my God. I just was where I was and didn't yet realize that I was on my way somewhere else. I was on my way home, but the way home turned out to be through the space that opened up when my heart broke.

As we live our lives, there are many fissures that crackle across the surface of the life we've lived up until now, the one we're trying to construct, or the one we're just trying to survive. With every fissure, every wound, every broken place, there's a space that opens. Much of the time, we find a way to medicate our hurts; we cover them over anything that insulates us: Facebook, media of any sort, codependent friendships, alcohol, romance novels, errands that need doing, closets that need organizing, hours in the gym. Most of those things are fine in themselves. But when we use them to "skin over" a crack that's opened up, then they keep us from letting Love fall in.

If we've listened for his words, if we've tried to see his face, if we've prayed and tried to press into the truth of him, then his words are there, ready to squeeze into the space we've opened up, no matter how narrow or uninviting. My friend Father Thomas says that Jesus stands outside the door of our hearts, like a beggar, knocking and asking us to let him in. If we open the door, he lunges in, and then he's like a thief. He steals your heart, taking all you have, rearranging everything, burning you up! You've opened the door to Love, and he's come to make a home of you—a home, where Love lives, and you finally get to be who you *are*, finally finished with trying to make yourself into who you think you're supposed to be. You are yourself in him, and he is your home.

But it's no good trying to put a sweet little "Jesus coat" over a great, gaping wound. Sometimes things hurt so badly, there's nothing to do but just try to take the next breath. To wake up in the morning, dreading another day you have to survive, and still putting your feet on the ground. Standing up. Going to make the sandwiches for the kids' lunches, or putting on the "armor" of your work clothes, and walking out the door. The movies tell us that heroes save lives, pick up lepers, or make peace among nations. But I've seen the most heroic people—the ones who make my eyes sting with tears for the beauty of them—just get up in the morning and make sure the children have the right P.E. uniform in their bags; they help pick up the pieces of a daughter's, or sister's, or friend's broken heart and bring a lasagna too; they take the chaos of the day and bring enough peace so that the people in their "home" find sanctuary, a place to take a breath before they have to dive back into the battle. There are many more heroes than we know. But maybe it's better to call them what they are: saints. Real saints, not dolled-up "perfect people" we burn small votive candles in front of. But ordinary people, who have "let the words fall in," who let Jesus burst in the broken places and burn them up, who stopped "knowing" who he was, and started looking for him where they didn't think he could be. Right in the middle of what breaks your heart.

I have a daughter with terrible epilepsy. She started having seizures when she was eight years old. I had taken her and her cousins to a summer art class and as I was standing outside in the parking lot talking to my sisters, the teacher came rushing out, saying, "Come quick! Something's happening to Cecilia!" I rushed to the door, and when I got there, I saw that she was having a grand mal seizure. She wasn't breathing. Her lips and her fingers were already starting to turn blue. You know how, when there's a crisis, you can have five to ten minutes worth of thought in a few seconds? As I was rushing to her side, I heard my own self saying (it was the Holy Spirit, of course, but he was talking to me in my voice), "This doesn't take God by surprise. I didn't wake up knowing that this would happen today. But God did. And he is already here. He is already kneeling next to my sweet girl, whispering words of love to her." As I knelt in the dirt, holding my beautiful, convulsing girl, I knew Jesus was with me. I felt a great quiet in me. A quiet I should not have felt in such a terrifying moment. But the Word was there, and he held me in his mercy. His mercy brought quiet, not certainty. As we rode in the ambulance to the hospital, I prayed, thanking God that Cecilia was alive, that I was not having to think about what dress I would bury her in. But then, there was another "word," a moment of dark illumination, when I knew, that even if I were having to think what dress to bury my girl in, I would still have to thank him for his mercy.

Is it not true? He either *is* merciful, or he's not. When we cannot see his mercy, is it because there is no mercy there?

Or is it because we do not know how to "see"? Kristin tells us that things don't "happen *to* us; they happen *for* us." Dear sisters, it's dark in the middle of heartbreak. There's no burning shrubbery telling us what in the world God is up to. There's no mystical carpet that carries us over the anguish and the fear and the horrible powerlessness. There is just Jesus, standing with us in the dark, whispering his words to us, mostly through very "ordinary" things. Jena, on a couch at Kristin's house at the Bible study class (the Word was there already, wasn't he?), surrounded by "sisters" who loved her, and praying words that she should not have been able to pray just a week after losing her husband—words she doesn't even remember praying. But they were words none of them would ever forget. Jena prayed from her broken heart the words that had dropped in, and all of them heard "Mercy."

Recognizing Mercy, and opening the door to him, is not easy. We have to be willing to confront our own assumptions about what God's compassion looks like. We have to be willing to see Jesus as he is, and not as we want him to be. When Cecilia was sixteen, her seizures were getting so bad that we decided to try brain surgery. We were in the hospital for two weeks. She had two surgeries; the second was a resection of a third of her right frontal lobe. Cecilia was her brave and gracious self throughout the grave and seemingly endless ordeal. For six months after her surgery, she didn't have any seizures. I recognized Jesus in this form, an answer to a mother's anguished prayer. She had been through *so much*! I was so grateful for his movement and his mercy in her life!

Then, on a dark night in November, my sister called. She had taken all the kids to a football game. When the phone rang, I knew. As I answered, I was already running toward the door. Cecilia had had a seizure and was probably going to need stitches. I wept and cried out in the car, all the way there, "Jesus, I trust in you! Jesus, I trust in you!" over and over again. This was mercy, too. I didn't *feel* trusting. I couldn't see how this could be mercy. I believed Jesus must be there, but where? The darkness closed in. In my mother's heart, right next to "Jesus is Lord," was an inescapable question: *Why?* I thought I knew him, but I couldn't find him in that darkness. My assumption about who he would be for us kept me from seeing him, even though he was standing right next to us the whole time.

Now, I know that on that dark night in November, our hearts broke, and the *real* Jesus fell in. That was five years ago, and I can't even begin to tell you how immensely beautiful he really is! Cecilia has been forged into an exquisite woman. She is so unerringly gracious, so deeply generous, selfless, and loving. She is one of the kindest, shyest people I know. You see, she was the one who hurt the most that night, the one whose hopes were shattered, as she let him fall into her broken heart. She let him come to her as he was, not as she wished him to be. And do you know what? The mercy he brought, the mercy he *is*, was infinitely more beautiful and life-giving than the narrow little kind I thought I wanted.

Kristin tells us that the key is gratitude. That is one of the great secrets of the spiritual life! To stand in front of what is, believing that Love is there, not necessarily in the "tragedy" itself, but in every space around it, dropping into our deepest hearts, if we'll let him. After Ceci started having seizures, some other neurological symptoms began. She spent ten months "asleep," only getting out of bed for maybe an hour a day. We didn't know what was happening. We tried everything! Finally, we found a medication meant for patients with serious narcolepsy, and she began to "wake up." Only a few months later, we were in a store buying her a bridesmaid's dress for my sister's wedding, and she had a seizure. She sliced her jaw open as she hit a glass display case. We went to the hospital in the ambulance, which she calls her "mobile home." We got her stitched up, and we were driving home. I was trying to think of what I should say to help her "meet" this yet another hard thing. I didn't want to be the "Eeyore" mom: "Oh no! Not another scar!" That would only help her feel like a victim. And I didn't want to be the "wasn't that an adventure!" mom, because that requires a lot of therapy later. While I was trying to decide what wise words I was going to bestow on her (OY!), Cecilia said, "Mom? Don't we believe that everything is mercy?"

Flabbergasted, I said, "Yes, baby. We do."

Then she said, "Well, I think we need to thank him for his mercy." Then she reached over, and grabbed my hand, and said, "Dear Jesus, thank you for the seizure today. Thank you for all the really kind people who helped us. Thank you that the brain surgery didn't work. Thank you for the ten months I couldn't wake up. Thank you that I'm behind in school. Thank you that my left shoulder is permanently dislocated because of all the seizures. Right now, it's too dark for me to see how this can be mercy. But I know that it must be. So, I thank you."

"The Lord is kind and merciful, slow to anger and great in compassion" (Psalm 103). Do you see? Can you hear how unimaginably beautiful his mercy really is? How can a young girl, facing such dense and incomprehensible darkness, become so open that she becomes the door grace rushes through? Cecilia held in herself the certainty that "everything is mercy." She had, through all she was asked to face, learned to say *yes* to so many *no*s, and her *yes* made it possible for her to come to the simple recognition that even mercy in its most incomprehensible form, requires our gratitude. In a beat-up, old SUV, on the way home from yet another visit to the hospital, I saw the unspeakable beauty of his luminous mercy, the depth of his compassion, and the truth of his kindness reflected in the face of my dear, young, handicapped girl. The joy and the beauty of it took my breath away. As the old song says, "How can we keep from singing?"

I am so grateful that he loved us enough to break our hearts so that he could fall in as he truly is—immense, compassionate, merciful, and loving beyond all imagining! Gratitude is, without a doubt, the door grace rushes through. Gratitude helps us, with him, to transform what should shatter us into what makes us whole. Won't you let him fall in through the broken places in your heart? Will you let him rush in by whispering your thanks, just because you believe his mercy must be there somewhere, even when it looks like it's nowhere? Will you let him be who he is for you, and love you as he is, and let go of the narrow, lifeless "Jesus doll" you've been carrying around? I promise you that the mercy, compassion, and kindness he brings will be the most priceless gifts of your life, and they will be priceless to everyone you share them with too.

Don't be afraid of your broken heart! Let Love fall in! He'll be your heart and your home!

saying yes to
FORGIVENESS

KRISTIN

---

orgiveness can be the biggest roadblock, or the biggest catalyst, to living in the fullness and freedom of Christ.

I know this is a tender subject. I know how hard it is to say *yes* to forgiveness. I have had a long journey on this subject, with lots of winding paths. I know this. I am not an expert. There is only one expert on forgiveness, and he is on the cross. However, I am a both a teacher and a student on the subject of forgiveness. I am an apprentice, an advocate, and generally a big fan.

This is a subject where we have to mentor each other, drawing each other out of resentment and bitterness and pulling each other along the path. In the area of forgiveness, I have to out myself up front and say that I have totally face-planted, mired in my own sin and ego. I have had my heart utterly broken, and have broken hearts. I have deceived, been deceived, been disappointed, and disappointed people I love. I have fallen short and gotten stuck. I know this much. Without forgiveness, we bottleneck both gratitude and grace, and we need both of these things for a life of freedom. Galatians 5:1 reminds us that it is for freedom's sake that we have been set free.

It might be tempting to brush by this subject, flip through this chapter and think that it applies more to "other people" than to you. I understand that. It's not easy to admit to the sharp edges and dirty corners in our hearts, the crap we carry around or stuff in the dark. But I'm going to ask you to hang in here with me. We're going to start with something, a little exercise I like to call the Unforgiveness Scan, searching for snags and scars. Take a deep breath. Clear your mind. Be fully here now.

> *Childhood. Perhaps you had a parent who didn't love you like you needed. Maybe you felt abandoned or unseen. Maybe you witnessed or experienced physical, verbal, or emotional abuse, alcoholism or another addiction. Maybe a sibling, friend, coworker excluded you, betrayed you, or hurt you. Maybe someone you dated, a fiancé, a spouse, or an ex-spouse broke your heart, your family, or your dreams. Someone at some point stole a piece of your innocence or your optimism, in some form or another. Maybe one of your own children or a daughter or son-in-law said things to you that you cannot unhear. Maybe someone hurt someone you love in a way that caused a deep crack in your soul. And certainly there are things you've done that you would give anything to go back and do differently. Ways that you yourself have hurt someone you love or someone you used to love, words from your mouth that cut someone to the core, decisions you made unconsciously or deceptively that were selfish and sinful, ways that you have fallen short of the person you want to be, the person you know you are deep down.*

Close your eyes for a second and feel whatever came to awareness for you right now, and hold it gently.

I want to honor that place in you, the past pain you received or caused. I want to tell you how sorry I am for that pain, how much compassion I have for you. And I want you to now hear these words—you've heard them thousands of times before, but I want you to hear them now as though for the first time:

> Our Father, who art in heaven, hallowed by thy name. Thy kingdom come, thy will be done, on earth as it is in heaven. Give us this day our daily bread and *forgive us our trespasses as we forgive those who trespass against us.* And lead us not into temptation, but deliver us from evil. For the kingdom and the power and the glory are yours now and forever. Amen.

Okay. Now we're ready to talk about forgiveness.

It's interesting to think about why we hold onto a grudge. We might think, "This is my story." "Who am I apart from this?" "You have *no idea* what this person did, and if you did, you would understand." It feels good to be angry, but it feels infinitely better to be healed. You know the old adage—"Hurt people hurt people." Well the inverse also applies: healed people heal people.

We think (mistakenly) that forgiving equals forgetting, or that we're saying that what happened to us was okay with us. Or that it's okay to continue the bad treatment, or even stay in that toxic or unhealthy relationship. Forgiveness simply means that we are choosing to unhook ourselves from past pain. We are choosing to change our focus, from darkness to light, turning back to God. You know the saying "What we focus on expands"? Well, if we focus on the pain, the past, bitterness, resentment, ugliness, betrayal, or trauma, they grow and continue to perpetuate and perpetrate. I'm in graduate school right now, studying psychology, so we learn a lot about neuroscience. Do you know that the mind/body connection is such that when your mind focuses on past trauma (or residual fear, anger, etc.), the body reacts as though it is happening right now, in the present moment? What does this do to our health? Stress levels and cortisol rise. The endocrine and nervous system are dysregulated. Risks for heart attack, stroke, and hypertension elevate.

So basically, we hurt once, and continue to hurt, sacrificing our health, happiness, peace, and well-being again and again and again.

It's time to stop the madness.

Let's say you agree. Okay, fine, I will try to forgive. So now what?

Forgiveness is a process, like salvation vs. sanctification. Salvation happens in an instant, but we have to work out our sanctification over a lifetime. It's like saying yes to getting engaged, but then there is the lifetime work of a sustaining a marriage. Like both of these things, the initial choice to say yes is our free will; we can choose obedience, choose love and light, choose to let go. But the higher power required to accomplish this is God's.

To be transformed by the renewal of our mind (Romans 12:2) implies that we have to change the way we think. Changing the way we think changes our emotions, which changes our actions and our choices, which ultimately changes our character and the sum of our entire life. I don't know about you, but I want to say *yes* to that.

It's one thing to *want* to do something, often another thing entirely to figure out exactly *how*. I don't have the answers for you, but I can tell you some practical things that have really helped me with areas of unforgiveness.

The first one I call the Forgiveness Marker, and it is a visual or mental cue that marks the split between then and now—the precise point when you chose to let go. One time mine was a smooth black stone I picked up as I ran along the beach and decided I had had enough with being resentful. Another time, I spotted a discarded can of pineapple juice against the wall as I was waiting in a long TSA line at the airport. I decided that there was specific baggage (we'll call him Joe—ha ha!) that I did not want to bring on this trip or carry ever again. After that point, every time I thought about him, I said, "Pineapple juice" to myself and it was such a bizarre thought that it made me smile and it actually worked to change my thought life. It jolted me out of a negative thought pattern and opened my heart and mind to better things. When my ex-husband told me his new girlfriend was pregnant, I knew I was at a crossroads between being bitter or being free. I wanted my kids to know that I welcomed their life, all of it. A dear friend suggested I start knitting a baby blanket, to be a visual representation of my feelings of openness and goodwill. My kids saw me knit that blanket in waiting rooms at the pediatrician's office, on airplanes, and sitting on our sofa. It took me nine months to knit that thing, and it wasn't particularly pretty, but I did welcome that sweet little baby and embrace his mother. Now I cannot imagine life any other way.

The next idea is something I got from Oswald Chambers: the Thirty Day Treatment. When you feel like you are stuck or at an impasse with a certain someone or a situation, this is a good one to try. Every day, for thirty days, whenever that person or situation comes into your mind, you send them or it a blessing and think about God instead. This may sound silly, but it is incredible. There may never be a change in the person or the situation, but there is an undeniable change in *you*. The change takes place in what Oswald calls the "workshop" of the heart and mind. Some people or circumstances in my life have taken me three rounds of the Thirty Day Treatment, but it has never failed me.

There are daily spiritual practices that increase our awareness and overall, ongoing ability to be open, patient, compassionate, and forgiving. I start my day with a prayer and meditation practice and go into my "workshop" by writing a list of intentions for the day. *I practice radical acceptance. I connect to God as Source and everything flows today. I let go, and my heart is at ease.* I love to meditate on the Serenity Prayer: "God grant me the serenity to accept the things I cannot change, courage to change the things I can, and the wisdom to know the difference."

I have a daily Gratitude practice. I make a quick list of ten things I'm thankful for and why. Over time, I have even been able to thank God for things I don't want—a difficult person or situation, frustrations, seemingly bad luck. I find that if I stay open, I can eventually see how he uses all of these things to weave a beautiful story.

I like to practice the Mirror Theory whenever I feel particularly reactive. The idea is that we react to things *because we know them.* When someone is rubbing me the wrong way and I find myself reacting to their selfishness, their ego, or their lack of authenticity, I ask myself to pause and look in the mirror. Some trait of theirs is bothering me so much because I know it—well. And I usually know it well because I have it in some form or another. This is not fun, but it gets easier. It helps so much to recognize our patterns and acknowledge our own areas for growth and change rather than finger-pointing where someone else needs to improve. We start to feel less like a victim and more like a victor.

I love the quote by the Greek poet Archilochos: "We don't rise to the level of our expectations, we fall to the level of our training."

It's up to us to say *yes* and train ourselves in the art of forgiveness.

SALLY

One of the many things I love about Kristin is that she doesn't dance around and try to decorate difficult things with magic sprinkles, little shiny words full of piety and platitudes. She doesn't call a brutal wound something else...like a "precious Jesus door." I've never heard her with a grieving friend, say, "God will never give you more than you can handle," because sometimes he does. She tells the truth. She calls things by their name, even if it's not a very pretty one. She doesn't try to cover up the parts that make her look bad. She doesn't pretend she's not afraid sometimes, just like the rest of us. But somehow along the way, she figured out that the truth was important, no matter how hard it was to see, and how much she wanted it to be something else. She believed that she was meant to live in freedom and she knew that faith was the only way to get there. And she loves fiercely! Which means she presses hard into the truth, knowing that somewhere in the middle of it, she'll find mercy. She's not afraid to call mercy by his name: Jesus.

Freedom is what happens when we finally recognize that the whole of life is, as Norman Cousins once said, "an adventure in forgiveness." By adventure, I don't mean the Carnival Cruise type. I mean the kind where you can fall off a cliff or get lost in an endless Amazonian forest. It's the kind of adventure that will cost you your life. Living into forgiveness sets you free and opens the door to compassion, fulfillment, love, and joy. Turning away from forgiveness traps you in a life you survive, where trust can't exist, loneliness, resentment, and self-pity never let you be, and love is crushingly conditional. Forgiving will be the hardest thing we'll ever be asked to do. But it's the one thing we have to do, or we'll always be a prisoner to our hurt. "To forgive is to set a prisoner free, and you discover that the prisoner was you" (Lewis Smedes).

I've been a prisoner in the jail of unforgiveness, where resentment, hurt, disappointment, pity, regret, and blame were the bars on my cell door. The thing of it is, I thought I *had* forgiven. But the truth was, time had passed and the "doings" of daily life had covered over the door, hiding my hurting "being" inside. The hurting was deep, next to my bones, burrowing inside, "making tunnels through every ground of confidence" (John O'Donohue, *To Bless the Space Between Us*). I didn't notice, or I just wasn't paying attention until, one day, I found myself in a place where I didn't know myself. I began to be aware of a deep anger toward my mother that kept showing up in weird moments. She and I seemed to have a good relationship, but then she would say something, or do something, and my anger would flash, completely out of sync with the situation. I wouldn't necessarily say anything or react outwardly, but I felt it wash over me, and it was a struggle to keep it leashed inside. Sometimes, it got loose, and she and I would have these arguments that left us both hurting. One of the signs of lack of forgiveness is feeling like a victim. I felt deeply hurt and victimized after these arguments. I truly loved my mother, so I was bewildered by this creeping, tunneling anger.

Years before, when I was ten years old, my mother and father divorced. Mother remarried a year later, and six months after that we moved from Texas to Alaska. She described the move as a "great adventure," but for me and my four brothers and sister, it meant we would only see our dad twice a year. We were heartbroken, but we were kids, and there was nothing we could do. I wrote my dad every day for a year after we moved. For each one of us, the wound of having "lost" our father was very deep. But the years passed, and the grief stopped tumbling me over. I thought I had "grown up" and forgiven. But forgiveness is a decision that requires action, deliberation, direction, and prayer. Time does *not* heal all wounds—they're just harder to see under all the layers of life we've deposited over the top of them. The same is true for the hurt that needs forgiving in us, and for the forgiveness we must seek for the wounds we have inflicted on others. The hurt can look like an Irish barrow, a gentle, lush green mound in the landscape of our being. But inside, it's a tomb, full of dark tunnels and bones. (Sorry for the creepy imagery!)

Early one morning, while I was praying, the barrow opened and I found myself in a dark place, full of "bones": resentments, hurts, anger, and disappointments that I thought had gone long ago. I was deeply angry at my mother for taking us away from dad. I had five children of my own, and we were in our own hard place, and I found

that I could not understand how a mother could rational-
ize taking five children away from their father. I tried to put
myself in her place so I could find some common understanding, but I knew I could never do what she had done.
If she had been truly sorry for doing it, maybe I could find
a way to generate enough compassion to forgive. But she
wasn't sorry. She still thought of it as the "great adventure," which made all of us mad every time we heard it. So,
if I couldn't forgive by "putting myself in her place," or by
responding to her heartfelt sorrow, how was I to forgive?

I prayed hard, making the decision to forgive, but not
knowing how to accomplish it. What I knew was that Jesus
came to forgive, and that he would be faithful in answer-
ing my heartfelt prayers. But I needed to be faithful in
praying them, like the persistent widow in Luke 18:1–8.
It was important not to try to cover the hurt over with
pious, powerless, "Jesus statements" like, "just let the forgiveness of Jesus into your heart." I'd heard that so many
times, but I had no idea what it actually meant to do such
a thing. What seemed important was to let what hurt,
hurt. Let the hurting itself be the reminder that I had to
keep praying. I needed to stand in front of Mercy as he
hung on the Cross, and have the courage to see what forgiveness cost. Instead of clinging to my wounds, I needed
to climb into his. St. Ignatius prayed (from the medieval
Anima Christi prayer), "*intra tua vulnera, absconde me*,"
"within thy wounds, hide me." I knew I was powerless, and
that Jesus needed to forgive in me, so that I could forgive
through him. So I crouched in the wound in his side, the

one St. Catherine of Siena called, "the door to his heart." In the dark, surrounded by him, I waited for him to draw me into his heart, and into a forgiveness I could not construct but could only receive as gift. I just kept praying, kept acknowledging my weakness, kept abandoning myself to him, and waited for him to be Creator—creating the forgiveness I could not even conceive.

I laughed when I read Kristin's description of the Thirty Day Treatment! It was precisely that! Every time I would think of being angry or resentful about Mom, I would remember that Jesus was working away, deep inside the barrow, excavating all the bones, all the hurts. I would press into him, reminding him of his promise, which in truth, was me reminding myself of his promise. He always keeps his promises!

To understand the promise kept for me, I have to tell you that I was given a gift. I didn't begin to recognize the gift until I was in college. But then it came to me very strongly, and I realized it had been there for a while. It is that I can feel other people's feelings, not just in a simple way, but almost as if I share their heart. I'm sure some of you also hold this capacity. I cherish this gift and know that it was from Jesus, for I never could have fashioned such a thing! I was on Kristin's "Ninety Day Treatment," almost to the day. I was working as a chaplain for hospice, and I received a very beautiful letter the eighty-ninth day. One of my patients, "Mrs. Dell," had been estranged from her daughters for almost twenty years. Mrs. Dell asked me to call them to tell them that she was dying. They both came two days later. For the next week, they stayed with their mother, having many conversations during the times she was conscious. The four of us would sit in Mrs. Dell's room, and she would tell stories to her girls about when they were young. We spoke of forgiveness, and they tried hard to get past the regret of the lost years. It was a little awkward in the beginning, but soon there was a great sense of peace and of love that settled in the old lady's room. After eight days, Mrs. Dell passed away, and her daughters were right there, each holding her hands. A week after her funeral, one of her daughters wrote me one of the most beautiful letters I have ever received. She said I was responsible for giving them back their mother; I had helped make them a family again. It wasn't true, of course. That was what the Holy Spirit was doing. But he let me have a small part of opening the door, so he could rush in.

As I read the letter, an astonishing recognition came over me! I realized that the gift I had been given was what he had used to crack open the door into Mrs. Dell's hurting family. But in a flash, I knew! I knew that he had come to deposit this priceless gift at a time when my heart had been "opened." He came through the fissures of my broken heart when I was ten years old.

Oh my! Oh my! I can't even write of it now, without crying. Jesus kept his promise, but so much more powerfully and beautifully than I could have ever conceived. He transformed the very thing that was the origin of my suffering into the birthplace of my gift! Do you see? I didn't need to "forgive" Mom in the same way, because it wasn't a hurting place, anymore. It was a place of rejoicing! Jesus

brought forgiveness and healing, transformation and resurrection all in the same moment. "How can I keep from
singing?" He had changed my "history"—not the circumstances, but how they lived in me. What had been a barrow,
became a garden, growing, living, fragrant, beautiful! I had
to learn to live into this transformation. I held in myself
many "habits" of smallness, and vestiges of resentments.
But he was with me, keeping faith and teaching me how
to praise and give thanks. Out of his immense generosity,
he continued to bring gifts. I came into a deep compassion and understanding for my mother, and of why she had
chosen what she did. We became closer than we had ever
been before. Jesus also showed me many areas in which I
had been petty and mean-spirited, clinging resentfully to
my hurts. He helped me to ask for forgiveness, and the gifts
of his healing and reconciliation continued until my mother's death last year. Richard Rohr wrote in *Breathing Under
Water*, "Forgiveness is to let go of our hope for a different
or better past." Jesus brought me into a forgiveness that
changed a bitter past into a better one.

Pope Benedict XVI wrote, "Forgiveness is not the denial
of a wrong, but a participation in the healing, transforming
love of God which reconciles and restores." In the prayer
Jesus taught us to pray, there are seven petitions. Six of
them are things that God does. Only one of them is something we must do, forgive. In Matthew's gospel (6:7–15),
he teaches us the Our Father. He makes only one commentary after the prayer. He says, "If you forgive others their
failings, your heavenly Father will forgive yours; but if you

do not forgive others, your Father will not forgive your failings either." I've always thought that sounded a little harsh, almost like a threat.

One time, my fiery redhead, Juliet, who was eleven years old at the time, and whom we called "Fire Ant" for good reason, was having a problem with one of the nuns teaching at our homeschooling cooperative. Sister had unjustly accused Juliet of something, and Jules was as angry as a whole nest of fire ants! I tried to clear things up, but Juliet was having none of it. Finally, in a fit of frustration, I said, "You need to forgive Sister because it says in the Bible that if you don't forgive, then God isn't going to forgive *you*."

Juliet got quiet. Then, looking at me through narrowed eyes, she said, "All right. I'll forgive her. But it's only to save my own skin!" It was fantastic! *She* was fantastic! Juliet hit on the sticking point of that passage. It sounds like the divine hammer is about to drop. But there is a much more beautiful truth woven through these words, only you have to stand in the right place to see it—sort of like a rainbow. I experienced the indescribable relief, thanksgiving, and joy of his forgiveness. I saw, I knew, I felt, him holding me with such tender mercy! Mercy wasn't an "idea" to me, anymore; it was arms, and breath, and words of love whispered into my being. The great commandment is that we are to love God as we love ourselves. The "loving God" part, we get. It's the loving ourselves part that we often let slide away. If Jesus is merciful to me, then I must be merciful with myself. I must be tender with myself. I need to be kind to the "small and weak girl" in me, because he has been kind to her.

Here is where the waves of mercy begin to radiate into life. It's really hard to hold someone else's feet to the fire when we've finally learned how to take our own out of the blaze. When mercy becomes real to us, and we let ourselves be loved, the compassion we step into for ourselves becomes the compassion we begin to hold for other people. The wonderful Maya Angelou once said, "I don't trust people who don't love themselves when they tell me 'I love you.' There is an African saying which says, 'Be careful when a naked person offers you a shirt.'" Until we learn to be gentle, merciful, and kind to ourselves, we're the "naked person." But once we're "fully clothed in Christ," awash in his forgiveness, alive in the power of his living mercy, then we have been transformed and resurrected. It is either true for us, or it is not, though we all have to live into the full truth of it.

Jesus' commentary on the Our Father cannot be seen as a petulant eight-year-old who's not going to let you have the toy he's holding until you give him the toy you're holding. It's this: If you can't find mercy for someone else's weakness, then you haven't found mercy for yourself. If you can't generate forgiveness for someone else's failings, then you haven't experienced the life-giving generation of forgiveness for your failings in yourself. But once you've experienced his mercy and his forgiveness, you are so transformed by the power of his love that you could never withhold your forgiveness from another. It would be like denying your very self, because he has become the center of who you are. St. Paul says, "Now this Lord is the Spirit, and where the Spirit of the Lord is, there is freedom.

And we, with our unveiled faces, reflecting like mirrors the brightness of the Lord, all grow brighter and brighter as we become the image we reflect; this is the work of the Lord who is Spirit" (2 Corinthians 3:16–18).

Finally, let me say that our holiness is bound up in forgiveness. Sister Ann Shields, in a talk on intercession, described the most beautiful expression of the power of forgiveness and intercession I have ever heard. It was a prayer, written on a little scrap of paper, and found on the dead body of a little girl when the Ravensbruck concentration camp was liberated at the end of the Second World War. The prayer was not signed, nor do we know if the one praying it was a Jew or a Christian. What we do know, is that she was a saint, for she prayed the prayer Jesus lived with his life.

> O Lord, remember not only the men and women
> of good will, but also those of ill will. But do not
> remember all the suffering they have inflicted on
> us, remember the fruits we have bought, because
> of this suffering—our comradeship, our loyalty, our
> humility, our courage, our generosity, the greatness
> of heart that has grown out of all of this, and when
> they come to judgment, let all the fruits we have
> borne be their forgiveness.

May we come to live the truth of forgiveness that brings, into our wounded families, and our hurting world, a love capable of such breathtaking transformation. Amen.

saying yes to

HEALING

KRISTIN

We all have areas of our heart or our health that need healing. I believe in the depths of my heart that Jesus heals today as much or more than he did when he walked the earth doing miracles in person. The problem is often that we don't know how to cooperate or collaborate in our own healing. So how do we say *yes* to being healed?

Let's look at a few stories to help us get a better understanding.

DO WE WANT TO BE WELL?

In John chapter 5, we read about Jesus healing a man who had been ill for thirty-eight years. And he healed him on a Sunday, which caused quite a Sabbath scuttlebutt. When Jesus saw him lying there, he asked this question: "Do you want to be well?" This question mystified me at first. This guy has been sick for thirty-eight years—*of course* he wants to be well. What else would he want? Jesus knows everything; so surely he knows this. But yet he asks. Why?

If we are completely honest with ourselves and each other, we might admit that there have been times where we haven't truly wanted to "get well." There have been times when we have told our sad, woe-is-me stories to anyone who would listen. In fact, we might have told them so many times that the story became kind of a sick identity. The way we affectionately talk about "my cold," "my sciatica," "my cancer," or "my divorce." We use the possessive "my" because we have begun to own it, to identify with it. If we aren't careful, our story can become our *story*. Our tune can become our theme song. Jesus knows this about us; he knows our weak humanity and our tendency to play the victim. He knows it can fill a misplaced need for attention or comfort when we have forgotten to go to him first to get our needs met. So, in his infinite tenderness and wisdom, he asks that very hard and personal question. Of course, he already knows the answer when he asks it, but he must want us to answer and think about it for ourselves.

So. We return to the question. Do we want to be well? That is a *yes* that requires some introspection—and sometimes some brutal honesty. Do we want to be healed more than we want to hold on to this pain? Are we willing to let go of something old or familiar in order to grasp something new or unknown? This question is tougher and deeper than it seems on the surface. We have to take some time with it and wrestle with it a little (or a lot).

This is step one of cooperating in our healing.

PICK UP THAT MAT
The story continues with the sick man. In John 5, verse 7, he goes on to give Jesus excuses for why he hasn't done anything to get better, why he doesn't take care of himself. "I have no one to put me in the pool...Someone always gets there before me!" This sounds pretty whiny to me, but the guy has been sick for thirty-eight years, so I can imag-

ine he is not his best self. But then, we are never at our best when we remain unhealed, are we? If I am more honest, I can tell you plenty of times I have given God my own whiny excuses for why I haven't helped myself. *I'm so tired. I can't afford it. I'm lonely. No one cares. I'm too broken. I'm abandoned. People hurt me. I'm too far gone.* We blame other people and outside circumstances for why we're not working on an inside job.

Next Jesus makes a very bold statement in verse 8: "Rise, take up your mat, and walk."

If this isn't a holy chiding, a pull-yourself-up-by-your-bootstraps moment, I don't know what is. In this simple directive, Jesus actually gives quite a bit of instruction. So this becomes step two of saying *yes* to healing. After we decide if we truly *want* to be healed (step one), then we have to get off our asses (sorry) and *do* something. We have to want our healing, and we have to cooperate with God by contributing to it. We can't just sit around for thirty-eight years and wait for him to do everything all by himself. He can do everything, no question about that, but he wants to see a little elbow grease on our part. I imagine him thinking, *Work with me, people.*

"Immediately, the man became well, took up his mat, and walked." Read that again. The man became well *as he stood up.* Notice he didn't become well and feel better and then try to stand. He did something bold, he acted upon the healing promise of Jesus as though it were already real, and his belief combined with action became the catalyst for the healing to occur.

BELIEF + ACTION = HEALING

This makes perfect sense when you think about it, because belief in action is just another way of describing faith.

If you really want to say *yes* to being healed, and I mean really want it, then what is God calling you to do about it? If you know and haven't done it, then get after it now. If you don't know or aren't sure, then stay put on your mat a little while longer while you ask what to do next.

A LITTLE HELP FROM OUR FRIENDS

In Mark chapter 2, we get another important insight about healing. This is the story of Jesus healing a paralytic. Jesus healed a lot of people, but this story stands out to me the most. A huge crowd had gathered in Capernaum to listen to Jesus preach, and probably hoping to catch a few miracles as long as he was in town. Four friends hear about Jesus and decide to take their paralyzed friend. I imagine him probably saying, "No, seriously guys, it's okay. Go on without me. I'll just hang out at home tonight and read or binge a little Netflix." They aren't having any of that. So they drag their friend out, probably literally, and when they get close to the spot, there is no way to get near Jesus because of all the people.

But these are real friends, so they are not thwarted or intimidated by obstacles. They don't give up.

They yank their friend up *onto the roof of the building, cut a hole* in the roof, and lower their buddy down on a mat. Can you imagine? It had to be the ancient-day equivalent of a rock star entering a concert by dropping onto the stage on a cable.

Verse 5 says this: "When Jesus saw their faith, he said to the paralytic, 'Child, your sins are forgiven.'"

When Jesus saw their faith. This makes me weep. I have had low, broken, unhealed times in my life when I was too weak, too hopeless, or too tired to do much of anything to assist in my own healing. There have been times when I only had the energy to utter one tiny, tear-filled prayer: God Help Me. Like this lucky man, I have friends who would lower me through a roof to get to Jesus. I have friends who have believed in my healing, who have believed in my worth, who have believed in a bright future for me and for my children when all I could do was cry and see nothing. *They believed when I could not.* And when Jesus saw their faith, he started to heal me.

The point is this. We need faithful friends. We need friends who believe and drag us to God when we've got nothing. And we need to be hope and faith to our friends in this way as well. We need to tenaciously and tenderly pull each other along. So this becomes step three in saying *yes* to healing: ask for help, and help others, whenever you can.

ANOTHER KEY POINT

I didn't want to skip over this part of verse 5, but I had to finish obsessing over these friends first. After Jesus is impressed by the faithful friends; he turns to the paralyzed one and says, "Your sins are forgiven." Wait, that's interesting isn't it? He doesn't say, "Here, let me fix your legs or your spine so you can walk." Instead he talks about forgiveness.

Hmmmm, why do you think this is?

To me, this means that a significant portion of the things that really need healing in our lives come from sin. When we don't ask for forgiveness, when we don't offer it, when we don't receive it and believe we are forgiven, when we hold onto bitterness and resentment and pain—we get sick. Truly. If you have ever been in a place of unforgiveness, you know this is so true. You feel just awful.

Step four in saying *yes* to healing means we need to reflect and consider the possibility that sin or areas of unforgiveness are contributing to our inability to get healed or healthy. More on that in the next chapter. ▪

SALLY

I love Kristin's steps to healing! They're helpful, truthful, hopeful, and practical. She doesn't present God's healing as a "sparkly cloud" descending on us, or a traveling preacher laying hands on us, and "claiming" our healing. We have to really want healing, be willing to *do* something about it (cooperate with him), ask for help from people we love and people who know what they're talking about, and then recognize what's making us "sick."

Here's the truth. Jesus heals. It's what he does because it's who he is. His love creates us; it makes us whole. Part of the deep truth is that it is precisely in those places where we are broken, the "hurting parts" of us, where we finally allow ourselves to be vulnerable enough to let Jesus in. The rest of the time, we work very hard at being in control. That's why St. Paul says, "My grace is enough for you, for my strength is made perfect through your weakness" (2 Corinthians 12:9). Jesus' strength is the power of his love to heal and save. And where can we meet him in his saving, healing love? It's where we have come to the end of ourselves, where we know we have no power. It's in our weakness. It's in the places we need healing the most.

But we are like the children of Israel, looking for a Savior who is a conquering king. They were expecting another King David. I've been like them so many times! I'm so ready to give fealty to the One who comes to conquer the occupying force that oppresses me—not the Romans, in this case, but my weaknesses, my afflictions, my failings, my sin. I want to give him my life and then let him be the king, the one who comes in and sweeps them all away through his powerful love and salvation. Then, I think, I can live as I was called to live, a shining witness to his saving love. I can be a great warrior for him in the world! Isn't that what I'm meant to be, after all?

But, though Jesus is the King, he is not the king we expect. Though he is our Savior, he doesn't save through ostentatious acts of divine power. He comes as a child, born in a tiny town, in a cave where they keep the animals, to parents who are "nobodies." He is God, but he comes to us in the most humble way. Jesus hides the immensity of his divinity in the smallness of his humanity. It's what he does with us; he brings his divinity into our weak, hurting humanness. He comes to us this way so that he can stand with us, as one of us, to hold in himself our sufferings, our failings, our shame, our disappointments, our anguish, our sin. He comes to save us and heal us from our sin and weakness, not as a conquering king, but as our brother, our lover, our most beloved friend—our Savior. He saves us by loving us and by drawing us *through* our sin and brokenness—*not* letting us avoid it by taking us over it, or around it. He takes us *into* it. He stands with me in my brokenness and failings so that my failing becomes his Way, the door through which the immensity of his mercy enters the deep places of my hurt, my heart, and my being. I am not saved because he "conquers" my sin (at least, not the way

I always thought). In his great humility, and unfailing love and tenderness, he gently asks me to press into the truth of my grave weaknesses, my crippling sin, and my un-healed wounds. He asks me to meet them because that is where I will meet him.

There's something really important to know about healing: it costs Jesus his life. In the beginning of Mark's gospel, Jesus heals a leper.

> A leper came running up to Jesus, and pleaded on
> his knees, "If you wish, you can heal me." Moved
> with compassion, Jesus stretched out his hand and
> touched him. "Of course I want to!" he said. "Be
> healed!" And the leprosy left him at once.
> *Mark 1:40–42*

At first, this seems like just a simple story of Jesus' "immense divinity" curing a sick man. But if we look closer, it's much more beautiful. First, it took great courage for the leper to come running up. Lepers were driven out. They had to bang clay pots and yell "unclean!" everywhere they went, so people could run away. They were thrown out of their communities, their families, and had to live with other people who were slowly becoming more and more horrifying, until they finally died, suffering, disfigured, and alone. The leper had the courage to come to Jesus and ask for healing. Then, something beautiful, that we might miss if we're not paying attention. Jesus was moved with compassion, and he touched the man. Can you imagine? It was probably the first time in years anyone had touched him. Jesus expressed his love in his deep look of compassion, his miraculous touch, the expression of his tender desire to heal, "Of course I want to!" And finally, he spoke the words of healing.

But here is the question we don't think to ask: Where did the leprosy go? Was it just a kind of "divine/magical" Harry Potter moment—"expelliamus!"—and then the disease disappeared? No. The leprosy didn't "disappear." Jesus took it into himself. He *became* a leper, though he did not show the external signs of it. He held it in his deepest self. This is the infinitely beautiful encounter with Love who saves, the Love who heals. For, at the moment Jesus pronounced the words of healing, he condemned himself to death. The only way the leprosy would be truly and finally gone was when it died with him on the Cross. That is what the love of God looks like—healing—so filled with love and longing, running so deeply into his heart and being and Divinity, he's willing to die for it.

Now, we're back to asking why we would be content with the kind of "cheap healing" we think we want. Let's think of it this way, for a minute (part of the "pretend" is that we are happily married. If that's not true, the same principle can apply to other significant relationships.) There is a certain "movement" in falling in love. It begins simply, like a few beautiful notes. Then, the encounters become more deliberate, and the notes gather into a lovely, distant tune. The encounters become more meaningful, penetrating your heart in deeper and deeper ways. The song gathers beauty, and fills your mind and heart and body. One day, you recognize that the melody has woven itself into the both of you and has become a kind of breath that sustains and fills you both. You marry, not for the sake of convention, but because you have found your home in the other, and you have made a home for them in you.

In the story of love, the wedding is not the beginning or the end. What would it mean to meet someone and then marry him the next day? You would have had no time to know each other, to discover what was splendid, to recognize the goodness and beauty of the other. You would have had no time to forge your friendship, to learn to count on each other, or to lean into each other when things were hard. You wouldn't know that when your heart was broken, the other would stand with you to hold the pieces of it until you could put it back together again. The love and fidelity that you promise in a marriage ceremony would only be abstract ideas, not something that had become a part of you, something that helped you to be brave, something that gave your life meaning and joy, something that generated life and light and love.

The story of healing is a love story. Healing is our heart being beckoned by Love himself. It is a progression of knowing, a movement of recognition. Each encounter becomes a place where love and trust are being born.

Do you remember the story of Jesus healing the blind man in Mark? It's a rather strange one. The people brought a blind man to Jesus to heal. He took dirt and his spit, and rubbed them on the man's eyes, then asked, "Can you see anything?" The man, who was beginning to see said, "I can see people walking around. They look like trees." So Jesus put his hands on the man's eyes again, and at last, he could see clearly. Then Jesus sent him home (Mark 8:22). Jesus' healing of the blind man was a "progressive healing." He took what was humble: the dirt; dirt was what we were made of in the beginning (Genesis 2:7), which is significant here because Jesus is about to "remake" this powerless blind man. Jesus then takes himself, his spit, to make mud to put on the man's eyes. This too is important, for in this case, it is his spit he uses to heal. Later in the love story, he will use his blood. The man's sight begins to come back. And Jesus is right there with him, waiting to lay his hands on him to heal him entirely. To heal him so that he can finally "go home."

I have a dear friend who has struggled with addiction for most of his adult life. He came to me weeping one day, asking me why, if he wanted healing so much, and he kept praying and praying, why was God "silent"? Why did God seem to be leaving him in this daily anguish when he was trying so hard, and praying so much? You cannot say to him, "You're in the middle of a love story." No. In that moment, you can only love him and stand with him. You can only be quiet enough to "hear" him and let your heart break with him. It's not always best to have "answers." Sometimes, your arms and your tears are the most priceless gifts you can give to a hurting one. And of course, you pray for all you're worth! Because as Christians, we believe that Love is on the way!

He's sober now, but it was bone-crushingly hard to get there. The Twelve-Step process was the door he went through to live his way into his healing. One day at a time, one step at a time, he began to find Love. It seems strange to describe it that way, but he had "medicated" himself because he didn't think he was worth seeing, worth knowing, worth loving. This journey into healing wasn't about progressing to a place where he could feel "all better." This journey, as is true for most healing, was a "geological" one. It was about depth, not distance. It required going deep, moving through layer upon layer of disappointments, woundedness, rejection, abandonment...all of it. Coming to understand our hurt and our weakness, not as an idea, but as a presence. It is not the "story" we tell about our life. It's discovering that the purpose of our life is to find Love—love who is there, buried deep under the aching layers of life's sediment. Jesus isn't waiting for us to dig ourselves out of the hurt we're in and the mess we've made. He's right there, seeing us, loving us, waiting for us to let him give us his mercy.

My sober friend became a "geologist." Not alone, but with friends, a sponsor, people who loved him, his faith, and with a willingness to just meet the day as it came. He excavated the layers of hurt that had entombed him. Now, he is happy, joyful, and free! He is humble and merciful because that's what happens when you come to know that you are seen and known and loved for who you are. He is one of the most beautiful people I know, and he never could have gotten there if he hadn't been "sick." He is a grateful alcoholic, one who doesn't relish the addiction but knows that the journey of excavation, required because his life had become "unmanageable," led him into the unspeakable joy of finding he was worth loving, worth saving. That he was worth dying for! That discovery brought him life and resurrection. His halting, trembling steps, one after another, became his great "love story," the story of his healing, the story of mercy buried deep in all of us but ready to burst into life when we're ready to dig deep for it. Will we hold onto the "story" we've made of our life and our hurting? Or will we let a bigger story grab hold, and set us free? Maybe it's time to stop hoping for "cheap healing" and begin, with Jesus, the work of healing that brings us resurrection.

One final note on healing. Sometimes it doesn't look the way we expect it to. Sometimes being healed means you're still going to walk with a limp, if you know what I mean. Jesus told the paralyzed man to "pick up your mat and walk." Why ask him to take his mat? That poor man was probably sick to death of that mat! But Jesus asked him to pick it up. Was the Creator of the Universe just a fastidious housekeeper? I'm sure Mary taught him well, but that may have been taking it a bit far! Actually, I think Jesus asked him to pick up his mat because that was going to be his "sign" to all the world that he had been healed! Don't you think it became his priceless "evidence of grace"? My beautiful friend is sober, but he carries the "mat" of his addiction with him. Not as a badge, or a bid for affirmation, but as a witness to the immense power of God, found in mercy and in truth.

So, God always heals—when we ask and permit him to. But we must remember to let him be God. God heals. God loves. God saves. We must allow him to love us, heal us, and save us as only he knows, in the most loving, most life-giving way. If it doesn't "look like" we wanted it to, then maybe we need to "see" the possibility of it being our "mat"—our own priceless evidence of grace, our witness to his healing and resurrection.

CHAPTER 8

saying yes to
TRANSFORMATION

KRISTIN

And I am sure of this, that he who began
a good work in you will see it to completion
at the day of Jesus Christ. *Philippians 1:6*

L ike Saint Paul, *I am also sure of this.* I love the idea that God loves us just as we are but also loves us too much to leave us where we are. He has bigger and better things in mind. He knows our blueprint because he designed us. He knows our story because he penned it. He knows our destiny, because he died for it. We are a work in progress, darlings, all of us. We are on the path of revelation, transformation, and freedom. Bit by bit, day by day, month by month, season by season, year after year, God is bringing us into our fullest identity with him. Through forgiveness and healing, old debris and other clogs loosen and fall away. Through obedience, faithfulness, and love, we forge new pathways and reach new destinations along the way.

May our hearts overflow with awareness and gratitude like Mary, and may we say, "The Mighty One has done great things for me, and holy is his name" (Luke 1:49).

These great things are *already happening for you.* If you can't feel them, or see the harvest yet, it's probably still sowing season. After you have spent many seasons farming life with God, the sowing season becomes as much or more fun than the harvest—because it's a chance to work alongside God and anticipate the abundance and blessing of the crops. There is nothing more exciting to me than rolling up my sleeves and starting to prepare a new field in my life, turning soil, removing rocks and weeds, and fertilizing the future fertile ground. It hasn't always been this way for me. I used to hate this season. It's messy, hard work, and I can see now that I did not fully trust the Farmer or his Almanac. I didn't trust his timing, his weather patterns, or his hard freezes. I didn't trust the fact that even his wildfires in my life had purpose: to burn up the old and use the ash to compost and fertilize the new. When I couldn't see something immediately, I assumed it wasn't there.

But let's think about this. Let's think about a seed.

A seed is a tiny promise; it contains all the material and hope needed for new life. We dig deep and bury that seed deep underground. We cover it with earth. We water it and pray for sunshine to warm the ground. The seed is completely unseen, underground, in the dark, which is how it germinates. At just the proper time, unbeknownst to us, it starts to burst and take root. It has to push its way through the soil and propel itself toward the light. And at some point, much to the planter's delight, it bursts through the topsoil and a tiny shoot emerges, ready to be nourished and grow.

Our dreams, our destiny, and the desires of our hearts are these seeds.

In order to cultivate our harvests and our gardens, we have to trust God's timing and his seasons. We have to trust God to transform us so we are ready to reap when the harvest is ready. We can't dig up seeds, yank them into the light, and pry them open to see if they are growing. Instead, we prepare the field, water the earth, watch the weather, and pray for the harvest. We wait expectantly and faithfully for God's abundance.

We have this fear of the dark. We want to uncover and expose our seeds. We want to roll stones away from tombs. We want to pry buds open because we can't wait to see the color of the flower. But our transformation doesn't work this way. The struggle is what creates the bloom.

My mother, Ethel, was a kindergarten teacher for most of her life. One of her favorite lessons was the hatching of the eggs in the incubator in her classroom. The way she complained about it, you might never guess it was her favorite, but it was. She had to go up to school on weekends to turn the eggs and check the light that kept the eggs warm in the terrarium. She had to constantly remind impatient tiny hands not to reach in and try to crack open the eggs. It was a lesson about life, a lesson about patience, and a lesson about struggle. You see, if one of her kids cracked an egg open prematurely, the chick would die. Even if the kids could see the tiny, fragile beak pecking away at the cracked shell, they were NOT ALLOWED to reach in and help them out. *The strength they needed to survive was born in the act of pecking their way out of the dark.*

Without the struggle on the inside, in the dark, the little creature would have no hope of making it on the outside—and *we are exactly the same way*. We have to struggle with our transformation. We have to be willing to remain, at times, in the dark places for as long as it takes for God to work out the changes needed in us. We have to collaborate with him in our renovation *and* our release. Our freedom is born here. Oftentimes we have to be willing to break wide open like the seed, or peck our way out like the fragile little chick, in order to experience new life.

> So, whoever is in Christ is a new creation:
> the old things have passed away; behold,
> new things have come. *2 Corinthians 5:17* ▪

SALLY

I t's so funny that Kristin and I, though it took a while to find each other, discovered that, even though our lives were different from the outside, we had found the same beautiful God *inside*. Lessons that had been important for her were important for me too. Kristin's mom let her kids see the miracle of a wee chick hatching and how important it was for the chick to struggle out on its own. "Helping" them wasn't helping them at all. I learned that lesson, too.

When I was a kid, I had a science teacher whose heart was in the right place, but who clearly wasn't firing on all cylinders. One of the "projects" she had scattered around the room was a glass mason jar, with a stick inside and the chrysalis of a monarch butterfly hanging from it. One day, our class noticed that the butterfly was trying to emerge from the sac. It was almost excruciating to watch; the struggle was so torturous! We all sat, transfixed. The teacher, though, was getting a little impatient. The emergence was extending into the next period, and she wanted to arrive at the finale. So she very took some small scissors, and carefully "helped" the butterfly out of the chrysalis. It clung to the stick, and we all breathlessly waited for its wings to begin to expand. But nothing really happened. It just kept walking up and down the stick, with two droopy orange and black "stumps," dragging behind it. The teacher finally let it go in the side yard of the school, and we watched it march away, with as much deliberation as it could muster.

It turns out that the tremendous struggle the butterfly must go through to emerge from the chrysalis is what makes it possible for its wings to expand. As it struggles, the fluid from its body is pushed into its wings, so that when it emerges, the wings, full of fluid, can expand and then harden. The butterfly then flies into its own brief destiny. Without the struggle, the wings can't expand, and it will never fly.

And there it is. The transformation that leads to freedom is a struggle. It *has* to be, or we would never have the ability to "fly." I know very well that if I didn't have to face difficult things, or recognize parts of myself that were petty and selfish, I would probably be content to stay where I am. Most of the time, I am pressed into change, forced into opening myself into another way to see and understand and act. A lot of the time, I confess, I don't go willingly. Thank God, literally, he doesn't let me stay in my smallness. He asks me to struggle, to fight, so I can emerge out of what keeps me narrow, all those things that keep me "in the tomb"—my thoughts about myself and my unworthiness, my worry over what I'm "supposed" to be doing with my life, my anguish over my sin and weakness, my bitterness over the hurts I carry, my confusion when he seems to say "no" to something that seems essential to my happiness. All of these things keep me bound up in the smallness of my own history, my own expectations, and my own assumptions.

Here is what I've come to *know*...he loves me too much to leave me there, crouching in that dark little tomb. He wants me to "become myself" and find the fulfillment, freedom, and joy he has for me. The story of the Transfiguration of Jesus seems like just one of the "miracle stories" in the Bible. But everything in Scripture echoes truth in our own lives. Jesus goes to the top of the mountain, and he is transfigured. "His face shone like the sun, and his clothes became as white as the light" (Matthew 17:2). The Father speaks, "This is my beloved Son. Listen to him." We describe this miracle as "transfiguration," but really, Jesus was simply "revealed" in that moment in front of the apostles. They got to see who he always had been: the Son of God, shining in his glory, when they had thought he was "just a man."

Jesus loves us too much to leave us in the cold, dark tomb of our hurt, sin, shame, weakness, and fear. We describe it as transformation, and that is a very good way to understand it. But in a deeper sense, what he is really doing is helping us strip away what hides the incredibly beautiful truth of us—the woman who bears in herself the unrepeatable, unique masterpiece of his image and likeness, shining luminously across her face, her life, her self. What Jesus wishes to do, through our transformation, is to tear off what binds us, so that everyone may finally see the transfigured beauty of who we were all along—if we let him set us free.

Remember the raising of Lazarus (John 11:1–44)? Jesus weeps in front of the tomb. Have you ever wondered why? He knew he was about to raise Lazarus from the dead, so why did he weep? Because his heart was broken for his beloved who had suffered, died, and was in the tomb. Jesus suffers for us, too, for what has wounded us, what has made us suffer, what has seemed to "die" in us. He weeps because we are in a tomb carved out for us by our lives, and trauma, and fear, and crippling suffering and anxiety that's kept us bound up. "Lazarus, come out!" he cries. "Sally, come out!" "Kristin, come out!" "You, dear one, come out!" The stone is rolled away. Slowly, we shuffle out, smelly and encased in burial bindings. Jesus says, "Unbind her, let her go free!"

The process of our transformation is the process of being "unbound," of stripping away what was keeping us from being free. There is no point telling you that it will be easy. You know as well as I do that it won't. But how easy is it to stay in the tomb? Do we want to keep holding all that shame, guilt, condemnation, sin, and anguish? Do we want to keep "dressing up," trying to look like a "virtuous Christian woman" for everyone around us, when inside we worry that it's just a lie, a lie a few people know—the people in our house who see us at our worst, and others who have seen the ugliness we have inside us? So it will be painful to let Jesus strip away the burial coverings. It will be scary to let him show us the truth of our weaknesses when he rolls away the stone from the tomb, and his light comes flooding in. But if we let him, if we cooperate with him, it will be the beginning of *joy*!

> Now this Lord is the Spirit, and where the Spirit
> of the Lord is, there is freedom. And we, with our

unveiled faces, reflecting like mirrors the brightness
of the Lord, all grow brighter and brighter as we
become the image we reflect. This is the work of the
Lord who is Spirit. *2 Corinthians 3:16–18*

I'll finish with a story, a true one that changed my life. I
was co-hosting a drive time show on a Catholic radio net-
work. We were on-air three hours every morning. One
morning, we were interviewing this ultra pro-life guy, who
had started some program. So, I'll tell you that I'm very
pro-life; I don't think abortion is an answer. I think loving
the mother, and the father, is part of the answer. I think
teaching children to see how loved they are, and educating
them, is part of what we have to do. I think it's important
to take care of people who are hurting and to value each
one of them as if they were Jesus himself—all of the poor
and the elderly and the handicapped, and anyone who is
suffering and needs our help. I don't think killing someone
for a crime fixes the broken hearts, or the broken one who
"sinned." I'm pro-life—life in all its forms, from the beginning to the end. I think it's important for me to explain how
very pro-life I am. Because however "pro-life" this man said
he was, I didn't hear it in what he was saying: "Any woman
who would have an abortion is a murderer!" In the name
of Jesus, in the name of mercy, in the name of life, he spoke
these words of condemnation and of death. I took it as long
as I could, but then, I couldn't stand it anymore. I said,
"You know. Jesus loves these women. His heart is broken
for them! So many of these women made this terrifying

decision in a moment in which they were filled with fear. So many of them were surrounded by other people who cared about them, but were also filled with fear. Here's what I have experienced….you know a woman a long time before she tells you about an abortion. That's the secret women keep. But Jesus loves these women. He was there with them when they lay on the cold table under the glaring lights. He was there when they went home, hurting. He is there in the darkness, while they grieve and are ashamed. Every women I've known who had an abortion knows what their child's birthday would have been. Is Jesus not with these suffering ones? He longs for them to turn around and *see* how much he loves them. He longs to give them the forgiveness that he's been tenderly carrying for them. He longs to gather up the broken pieces of their hearts, so he can make them whole again. So that they can hear him whisper into their deepest selves, 'Behold! I make all things new!'"

Six months later, I was in Minneapolis giving a retreat, and afterward a woman came up to talk to me. She was all shiny! She told me that she had been listening to the radio in bed early in the morning, and had heard that interview. When I began to speak of Jesus' love, she told me that she fell out of the bed onto the floor, weeping. Sixteen years before, she had had an abortion, and she was sure that God was so disappointed in her that he turned his eyes away from her. That morning, she realized that he had been standing next to her bed every morning for sixteen years, waiting for her to let him love her. Waiting for her to let him give her the forgiveness that he was already carrying for her.

That afternoon, she called around to find a priest who would hear her confession and, God is merciful, she found a good priest. At the end of her confession, she wanted a big penance. Isn't that what we do? We know we don't earn his forgiveness, but still, we think if we do something hard, we're "helping him out." But this priest was so beautiful. He stood *"in persona Christi,"* in "the person of Christ," and he said, with such mercy, "You've been living your penance for the last sixteen years. Now, go and be free in the love and forgiveness of Jesus Christ!"

I just started to cry from the sheer, indescribable beauty of it! You see, that day, I saw Jesus standing in front of me, alive in the face of this beautiful woman, set free. She had been to Mass every day for six months! That morning, she had finally *let* Jesus love her! She let him transform that grievous wound of her sin into the door his mercy rushed through. She let him roll away the stone that was keeping her in the tomb of shame and condemnation and death, and she followed him into resurrection! I can promise you, everyone who encounters this beautiful, glorious, splendid, alive, compassionate woman—*everyone* who encounters her, *sees* the resurrection! Each one is so deeply served when they meet her, because she unveiled her face and has become the Image she reflects. Everyone she speaks to, everyone she holds, everybody she gathers up into her life, touches mercy, sees hope shining, and hears Love, who whispers, "Behold, I make all things new!"

So, my dear sisters, do you long for transformation and freedom? Then have courage, believe that he planted this longing in you and is already giving you the grace to begin to live it in your lives. Give him the gift he wishes beyond all others. Give him your weakness, your sin, your wounds. Let him transform them into a living encounter with his breathtaking mercy. Let him roll away the stone that keeps you in the tomb of your shame and guilt and deathly, brutal condemnation. Let him make you new.

Then, wake up in the morning, unveil your face, and step all shining into your new day. Say *yes* to love, to his gifts of grace. Let this day be an annunciation for you. Say *yes*, and let him be born again in you. Like Mary, you will begin to wake every morning in the excitement of what your *yes* is going to look like today! Each *yes* makes you brighter. Each *yes* turns you into the image you reflect. Each *yes* draws you into resurrection, where you will be filled to overflowing with gratitude, love, mercy, and joy! There is no greater service you can give to him, and no greater joy you can live in, than to *be* Christ for everyone you meet today.

Come on, beautiful sister! Let's do it together!

Let's say *yes!*

ALSO AVAILABLE FROM TWENTY-THIRD PUBLICATIONS

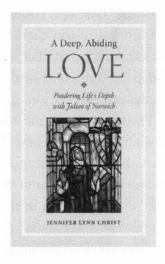

Holy Wind, Holy Fire

*Finding Your Vibrant Spirit
through Scripture*
PAMELA A. SMITH, SS.C.M.

The best way to experience the Spirit is to see what the Spirit does. In this beautiful book, Sr. Pamela invites us into a wonderful journey through the Old and New Testaments to catch glimpses of the Spirit at work. Reading, reflecting, and praying with this book will help to re-energize and reawaken us to the energy and joy that only the Holy Spirit can give.

136 PAGES | $14.95 | 5½" X 8½"
9781627853170

A Deep, Abiding Love

*Pondering Life's Depth
with Julian of Norwich*
JENNIFER LYNN CHRIST

Jennifer Christ draws parallels between Julian's times and ours and demonstrates how Julian's message of hope and joy in God's never-ending love for us can give us strength and hope. Spend time with this book—reading Julian's words, praying with them, pondering, and journaling, and letting her hope-filled message take root in your heart.

128 PAGES | $14.95 | 5½" X 8½"
9781627853156